Salsa Hips

A Novel

Joie Lamar

Also by Joie Lamar

Mambo Lips
Volume 1, Memoir Series

Salsa Hips
Volume 2, Memoir Series

Sapphoetry
Volume 1, Poetry Series

Cuarenta y Nueve
Curator and contributor. A Coffee table book in honour of the Pulse Massacre tragedy in Orlando, 2016. 49 contributors for 49 victims. *Coming to Brainspired Publishing 2022*

G
Volume 1, Crime Thriller Series

See Whores
Volume 2, Crime Thriller Series
Release February 2022

Dust Bunny Ben
1st Children's book; written and illustrated
Release June 2022

Salsa Hips - Volume 2 of Joie Lamar's Memoir Series
2nd Edition
Copyright © 2015 Joie Lamar
All rights reserved.

Brainspired Publishing cover design with Joie Lamar

No part of this series may be reproduced in any form or by any electronic or mechanical means including information storage and retrieval systems, without permission in writing from the author. The only exception is by a reviewer, who may quote short excerpts in review. This book is a work of fiction. Names, character, places, and incidents are products of the author's imagination or are used fictitiously. Any resemblance to actual persons, living or dead, events, or locales, is entirely coincidental.

Visit my website at www.joielamar.com

Brainspired Publishing

 A joint venture of *Brainchild Holdings Inc.* and *INspired Media Inc.*, Ontario, Canada

www.brainspiredpublishing.com

PAPERBACK ISBN: 978-1-7774054-1-0

Library and Archives Canada / Government of Canada Tel: 819-953-3997 or 1-866-578-7777

To anyone who wonders if I am writing about them.
I am.

Acknowledgements

My first adventure into writing has been a glorious one at that. Mambo Lips, volume 1 to this series, has not only been a cathartic experience but has also opened the door to so many opportunities. It remains the foreplay to this very raw and honest sequel that you now hold in your hands.

I want to thank the many pioneer readers of my novels. Your support and acknowledgement has made me feel like a genuine writer and has motivated me to keep creating. I have so many tales to tell and I endeavour to never let you down.

I also want to express my sincere appreciation and affection to my wife who is my pillar of strength during and after my writing. It is not easy living with a crazy creative mind but you do it so effortlessly and so elegantly. Your love is truly unconditional. Thank you, Natalie.

What can I say about someone who became my writing mentor and first publisher? There we sat in a dark bar in Toronto when I excitedly regurgitated my book ideas at you over a delicious glass of wine. I will forever be grateful for our chance encounter and how hard you worked towards my success. You taught me so much in so little time together. "Put that beautiful mind on paper." I now hear those words, your encouragement to me, in my head constantly, Mr. Jack Reams. Rest in peace my dear, sweet, and brilliant friend.

Last but not least, a huge thank you to my family and friends who continue to support my writing, my ideas and this new direction in my life. I am blessed and forever grateful.

Sword holder

1

A woman's body,
Divine.
Don't blush. Don't rush.
Like drinking wine.
Savour the taste.
Take your time.

The first time that I put my fingers inside another woman's vagina I knew that I had found the historically sought after Holy Grail. I can understand why and how it has been missed all of these years. I believe it is the horrendous nicknames this beautiful body part has somehow had attached to it over time. Perhaps, I suggest, as part of the master plan to hide it from mere mortals but I am after all, Aqua Girl.

The name vagina itself means sword holder. Why would anyone put a weapon in the space where most of us take our first breath? Not well thought out I say. I'm not here to change language but even "hoo-ha" sounds more inviting, and happy, I might add, than a place to pierce your Mama!

Let's explore some of the rest ~

Beaver? An ugly, foul toothed, animal that would deter anyone from giving it a proper kiss. Unfortunately, not kissing "the beaver" is a shortcoming that many wannabe lovers suffer from, and a huge complaint by most women. Surely that wood chewing animal would gnaw your face off! I say that name has *dammed* some great cunnilingus, pun intended.

Cunt? One of the few remaining words in the English language with the power to utterly shock or enrage someone. I could find no true etymology for the word or a meaning whatsoever. It does have some resemblance to similar words that mean wedge or to squeeze into. A deterrent to anyone suffering from claustrophobia, I would think. On a good note, I do join the ranks of great writers of modern literature such as James Joyce just by putting it into print, but I digress. It is safe to say that it is considered a disgusting word, again a name diverting us away from the true wonder of this flesh and nerve system from the Gods.

I suppose the name pussy gives you permission to pet it at the very least. We all, however, know that cats are aloof, independent, scratch and the second highest allergen known to human kind. Once again, a moniker that does not truly represent this miraculous passage to a woman's soul. I suspect that the ever hetero popular doggie position is not just an act of comfort but also a rebellious subconscious act of dog chasing cat.

That there are 50 ugly nicknames for female genitalia in just the English language alone is not as shocking as the last name I will touch upon. Camel toe is the ever so embarrassing reference to where the heavens have split a woman. Camels are also nasty, spitting, moody beasts of burden. This name from any angle is not conducive to healthy humping.

And so my quest for the Holy Grail, along with now knowing what these Mambo Lips were meant for, is the story of Salsa Hips. My message to the many seeking vaginal enlightenment is to forget all of the nasty nicknames designed to subconsciously lessen the beauty of a woman's lower lips.

More important than finding this ever illusive grail is the understanding that it is not just found in one place; or in one woman, to be more accurate. This is a journey. It is my quest to prove the premise that there is divinity in the female genitalia. This is the story of a Superhero mastering the God sent va-jay-jay in search of love.

Tony the tiger

2

You love my heart.
My sexual genius.
But I'm missing a part.
The glorious penis.

Jegana was 28 years old when we met at a lesbian club called La Femme in New York's famed Greenwich village. The more comfortable I became with myself, the more the village became my official stomping grounds.

La Femme was the place to party for the Latina lesbian crowd and dancing salsa or the hustle well, made you royalty. I was young, 20 to be exact, and painfully shy until I was on the dance floor. My whole persona changed when I danced. This life, although now comfortable for me, was still all new to me. I found my rhythm and my strength in this new world by moving to the music.

The club was always filled with a bevy of beautiful women. We dressed to the nines back then and these ladies made spectacular entrances in stiletto heels and provocative but tastefully revealing club wear. They had to walk past the bar to the back of the club where the dance floor, friends and attention awaited the best of them.

I was part of the butch crowd of that era and less dyke than the older crowd. My masculinity was natural and never over exaggerated. Still, I remained the ever proud mari-macho, as I was labeled in my youth. The single butches sat at the bar mingling and meeting friends, inviting these beautiful women to sit with them, or like me; shyly awaiting to ask just the right "fine girl" to dance in the back room. And by right girl I mean someone who did not expect more from me than jokes, dancing, a drink or a good high and sex, in that order.

To say she was exotic and gorgeous was an understatement. I felt the air leave my lungs when she entered the club but was cool enough not to outwardly gasp like everyone else feasting their eyes on her. Maybe that is why she crept in next to me to order a drink at the bar or maybe I just looked innocuous in comparison to the piranhas scoping her out. Whatever the reason, I will always remember her drink order. I was certain it was a come on line intended for me, and not just the name of a cocktail. "Harvey wall banger please." Her drink order dripped from her lips and caused the same reaction for everyone who was in ear shot of that sultry voice. We melted en masse. The women with a lot more experience than I started to hone in on her as she searched her purse to pay for a drink. I leaned in with my best thought at that moment. "Everyone is going to offer to buy you that drink in the next 10 seconds, but only I can give you a seat right in front of your glass, at the bar." She smiled up at me and I hoped right at that moment that I would not bomb out as the night's cheapskate. I would have bought her the drink too but made the split second call to offer her bar real estate, when it was 3 people deep, instead.

I slipped off of my bar stool and she sat down in front of her drink while I stood up next to her, one arm on the back of her chair, and my back to the competition that had been sitting next to me and staring at her. We looked like we were together at that moment so I made a point not to smother her in her first 10 minutes in the club. "I'll stand here to protect you from the ugly vultures. You let me know when to give you space." I whispered in her ear. She looked deeply into my eyes and crushed me with her next words. "You're just a baby, aren't you?" I deserved an academy award for my composure at that moment. That sentence translated to *'You're inexperienced, aren't you?'* but I faked my confidence, smiled and said "How old does someone have to be to give you a chair and protection in a club?" Jegana smiled, then laughed and introduced herself to me as Gigi. I told her that our names, said together, would be a tongue twister by the end of the night. We would go on to laugh a lot, over several cocktails, before I asked her to leave *our* bar stool and dance with me. I kept to my order of seduction, unintentionally.

I carried both of our drinks to the railing surrounding the dance floor in the back of the club. She followed closely with her hand in my back pocket as if we were already a couple. The DJ smoothly mixed *'Love is in the Air'* into play and we took to the dance floor without my having to ask. We hustled so well together. Fluidly. She was light on her feet and sexy to boot. I cannot recall how many songs we danced to, but we did so in succession, before hearing the DJ announce *"Last call for alcohol."* Gigi and I would close La Femme that early morning and jump into a cab to take her home afterwards.

"Can I invite you up for a night cap or coffee?" she asked, in front of her apartment complex. The ladies were so classy back then but what did that even mean? I did not drink coffee and at only 20 years old, a night cap sounded like a hat to me. I took my chances and agreed to a night cap fully expecting my hair to get messed up.

And so it did!

She made the most amazing *Cuba Libres*. I would learn that night caps are another name for cocktails and that Cuba Libre is another name for rum and coke. Well, not just rum and coke, but the perfect amount of lemon and lime, to cut the sweetness. Ironically, she herself had a similar formula.

Jegana was sexy and inviting, sassy enough so that you would never describe her as sweet, but loving just the same. She liked everything intimate a little rough. My lips bled from her biting kisses. Just when I would become angered by it, she would heal all wounds with her tongue. We made out savagely while she humped my leg to the point of ripping her nylons at the crotch. She began to take our clothes off, simultaneously, with great expertise. I was inexperienced so I can only believe that instinct took over when my hand found its way into her panties. She swallowed my hand to the wrist. I balled my hand into a fist to keep from hurting her and felt her shiver. We fucked like animals for hours and hours. Gigi liked to be fist fucked in every position. I was young, willing and a straight A student of the orgasm. Sunday morning, I awoke to the smell of coffee and sex. She was already in the kitchen making breakfast for me. Old school ways along with a good morning kiss and a wink. I ate quickly so that I could shower and head home. We exchanged our contact information and scheduled a date for the following week. After a long loving kiss that made me question why I was leaving so early, Gigi leaned in to say "I need a cock." instead of goodbye. Hoping I had heard wrong, I still asked "You're straight?" "No." she said "I need you to strap on next time, silly." "Oh sure." I tried to pretend and kissed her one last time before setting out to find my penis.

The Pink Pussycat was famous for its S&M paraphernalia, sex toys and all out Sodom & Gomorrah product portfolio but nothing could prepare you for actually walking into the store. I was hoping for a dark room with just enough light to see what you are buying, but not enough for any human contact. Instead, you are greeted by an ever so eager to help and knowledgeable staff. Every part of my being wanted to walk out when 'Suzy' introduced herself and asked how she could help me, but I could still feel Jegana biting my lips almost 3 days after *Cuba Libre* night. Under my breath and with a nervous squeak of a voice that I could just not butch up, I said "I'm looking for a strap on cock." I was reading straight from the to do list in my hand that also noted that it was my dear sweet Mamabuela's birthday. I am buying a penis on her birthday? Oh dear God. I joke about that with Suzy who, turns out, is a serious sex toy vendor. If she had only laughed loudly she would not have heard my knees knocking and I would be a much more relaxed customer. The bright lights seemed excessive just as Suzy placed a variety of dildos on the counter for me to consider, at such a busy time in the store. Had everyone in the village followed me into the sex shop this evening? I pondered never seeing Gigi again as Suzy explained each man sausage in detail. Finally, I chose what Suzy called a "realisdick", molded from an actual erect penis. She proceeded to explain what straps could support the nine-inch behemoth that I had selected.

I realized that I would be totally impressed and grateful for such attention to detail if I were buying an appliance. My red face subsided with these thoughts and I concentrated on buying that which would make me Gigi's love machine.

Dinner would be slightly awkward with the black unmarked bag that everyone in New York knew was from the Pink Pussycat hanging off of the back of my chair. Thank goodness Gigi found it both endearing and a turn on. She asked to look in the bag during dinner, excitedly, but I told her that a restaurant was no place for me to expose myself.

I'm sure that dinner was fabulous. I remember the tequila flowing followed by being naked, in her bed, with Tony strapped on.

Yes "Tony". It is traditional for lesbians to name their dildo(s), I would find out. It makes it easier to talk about them in public or in front of family such as *"I forgot to tell you Tony is coming over."* Mine would be named under pressure, looking down with it strapped on, and my Saint Anthony pendant on a chain around my neck just above it. My nanosecond of sacrilegious guilt disappeared when I realized that I also call for God when I'm having an orgasm. Sex had become my religion.

Gigi taught me every position known to man, woman and beast. Even under the influence of tequila and marijuana, I taught her endurance of tantric proportion.

We spent days on end covered in each others body fluids. The days turned into months and the months into a one-year anniversary. The relationship would organically flourish outside of sex and Gigi would become my constant companion, my woman. She was not smart, eloquent, educated or even interesting. She was beautiful, a great dancer and amazing in bed for the me of that time. My friends liked her for her party skills too.

Alberto was one of my closest friends. His nickname was Coqui, after the ever chirping frog of fame in Puerto Rico. True to his nickname, you could not stop him from opining about everything and anything. I loved him for this. Conversation never came to a stop with Coqui. And no matter how harsh his interpretation, he would always deliver it with a smile. A *'fuck you, I said it'* kind of honest grin. I had introduced him to Jegana early into our relationship and he chirped about her every time we met. "She is too fine." he often told me. "That kind of fine is trouble J." We laughed into our beers on many occasion as he tried to persuade me to start dating women who would attract less attention. "You know the not so pretty women are more grateful" he would joke. "She will either break your heart or someone will kill you for her man." Those words would ring true almost a year and a half into our being together, although not exactly as intended.

Gigi and I were having breakfast at 4:00am in the morning in a restaurant on West 7th street in the village, as was the norm for everyone leaving La Femme when it closed. The laughter and talking created a hum, interrupted by the sounds of plates slammed on to tables and orders yelled into the kitchen in Greek. She said "I need to talk to you" several times but I was preoccupied by making sure my food did not touch on the plate and quite upset that they did not remember my usual order and this request. Jegana leaned in to put her hand on my arm and the look on her face brought me back from being annoyed to her. "I need to tell you something Joie." she would repeat. "Tell me, what's wrong?" I was hungry, disturbed by my food touching and hoping that her need to tell me whatever it was did not interfere with my taking a bite of my food after finally getting it right on my plate. "I'm in love with you." Her words echoed with the crunch of bacon in my head. In an instant I was faced with a brand new life experience. Love with a woman. A woman in love with me, another woman. You never really give it any thought that being authentic to your lesbian calling would ultimately result in falling in love with a woman. My calling, at least at this point in my young life, was to experience the female body as my libido had been craving for all of these years. I was, however, very much aware that her feelings deserved validation even if I could not repeat them back to her. I think my exact response was "Wow."

Gigi had beautifully expressive jade green eyes that would somehow flicker orange flames when she was angry. I could see the embers. "Wow? That's your response?" she said loudly and above the hum, plates and Greek yelling. It seemed like every person in every booth in that restaurant was now looking at me. We were novella material and typical Latin drama; one sided love. "You're the only girl I am seeing." I went on to explain. "But you don't want me to lie, and say I love you, if I don't know that I do." We would end our breakfast quickly, in silence and take a long, awkward subway ride back to her place. We made love like it would be our last time, although it was not. I would try to fall in love with Jegana for the rest of our time together which was almost two years.

Her last straw was when she found a woman's telephone number in my pocket. I had no intention of calling that person but she was sure that I was cheating because I was not falling in love with her. Just the opposite. Sometimes you can pour your heart and soul into someone and still love will not come. The universe decides no matter how hard you try to control such things.

Our breakup was television worthy. We met at La Femme knowing that this particular night would be our last together. The chemistry was more pronounced than ever. We danced the night away, kissed passionately often and laughed together until our stomach muscles hurt. I wanted to take her home but she asked me not to. It was too painful she would say, for her. Like any good soap opera, the last kiss was perfect and felt by every part of our bodies. We were magically intertwined when she delivered her final love speech to me "You are the best. I can't imagine my life without you Joie, but I want you to find your heart. I will need the space and time to get over you." I cried for her sadness. I cried for losing the woman that I wanted to fall in love with. I cried for my not being able to love. She went home and left me crying on the dark dance floor in La Femme.

Two weeks later I would walk into Coqui's apartment to find her in bed with him. We were going to the beach and surfing together that morning. He forgot the outing and to lock his door. As it turns out, they had been together for more than a month and shortly after she told me she was in love with me. He did not jump off of her, nor was he startled, when he realized it was me. Quite opposite but true to his character, he said "I told you she would break your heart J." It was delivered with that *Fuck you I told you* grin too. And he was right, it killed me.

Saks 5th altercation

3

To reach me, follow the map.
Every hurt is a detour.
Every tear is a waterway.
Every success is a mountain.
Every death is a cliff.
Every friendship is a bridge.
Every love is a garden.
Every lesson is a road.

I would think of Gigi often. Mostly when intoxicated to be completely honest. I often wondered if this thinking about her was a precursor to falling in love. Should I have just repeated those words back to her? Is that how falling in love works? You repeat the words until your heart aligns with them? Maybe more painful then losing her was the truly hard pill to swallow, that the arms holding her now belonged to my good friend. Who did I miss more? It became a daily analysis in my mind for a while.

I did try to maintain a friendship with Coqui and ignore that he was with her. It was a complicated mental game that we played, and fascinating dynamics, retrospectively speaking. I played cool, calm, collected and totally at ease with their relationship. She became enraged at my composure and that I showed no signs of jealousy. He grew jealous over her anger at my lack of emotion. She found power in playing us against each other. I got over it quickly, leaving them to each other.

When the fog of all of this lifted I realized Tony was now my only true friend. Yes, Tony the dildo, although I preferred to call him a prosthetic pal. Together we would conquer the world that Gigi had released me back to. Only now, more informed and armed with nine inches. I carried my prosthetic pal with me every day and everywhere, in a knapsack, prepared to *'love you long time'* at any given moment. It never phased me that the same knapsack sometimes carried my son's binky or toy, alongside Tony. He was always in his velvet case with condoms. They came lubricated and kept everything clean, between women. The contents of my backpack personified who I was at that time; a mother, "A man woman" and adrift, forever identifying with the Seahorse.

The Duchess was just another little lesbian bar and dance club amongst the many in New York's Greenwich village but as the name of the place denotes, there was something regal about it. I was enamoured with being able to do some reading at the bar and having a cold beer after work. I was also quite the trivia game enthusiast. The game machines were made available, at the bar, up until the DJ arrived.

I was deep into my book and beer when Denise arrived and sat next to me at the bar. Tony was in tow, and in my knapsack as always, but it was Wednesday. It was still early evening and would be an early night home for me. The weather in New York was beautiful. It was spring, cool, bright and even the sounds of the city were sexy. The bartender asked me if I wanted another beer after taking her order for exactly the same brand. "Only if she is buying." I joked, shocking Denise. "Uh, yeah sure." She stumbled and went back to her purse for another bill to pay. "No, no, no, I was only kidding." The bartender seemed annoyed with me at this moment. She was so easily confused. "Yes, I'll have another Amstel Light and I will pay for my own." I was not intentionally trying to get her attention nor trying to pick her up. As it turned out, she was in a foul mood, and my humour distracted her in a good way. "Is that a joke book?" she asked sarcastically. "Only if you think the holocaust was funny." I countered. I was rereading *The Diary of Anne Frank* and showed her the cover. "Ah so you're a thinker." She said with an ever so thick 'New Yorican' accent. Denise wasn't gorgeous, she wasn't plain and she wasn't ugly. She was cute. And, I would find out, also ten years older than me. I will never know if it was the two beers, the fact that she was older, or just the incredible libido that I was blessed with but I found her to be extremely alluring. We spoke for another hour or so, later than I had intended to stAy at the bar. I told her about my fascinating trip to Amsterdam, as a child, where I visited Anne Frank's hiding place. I may have bored her with my passion for this story. How I am mesmerized by this young lady who writes about life while facing such uncertainty and imminent death. Denise humoured me that early evening.

Clearly we were lusting each other. I stole a very passionate kiss from her before she descended the subway stairs for her trip home. We set a date for dinner and dancing on Friday. I would have to bring my Mama flowers tonight. For both being late to pick up my son this evening, but also to retain her babysitting services for Friday.

Denise and I had agreed to meet in the city on Friday evening in front of Tio Pepes' Restaurant on west 4th Street at 7:00pm. I waited with bated breath and one red rose. She showed up wearing the slinkiest black dress and looking much hotter than I remembered her being at the bar. I regretted leaving Tony at home as soon as I saw her but I had dressed up too and would have no place to carry him. She was so grateful for the rose. More than normal. Like a woman who had not been courted in a very long time, or ever. Her hello kiss was warm and perfectly placed.

Tio Pepes was THE date restaurant of its time. The food was beautiful, if you ever actually made it to finishing a meal. The back grotto room was incredibly romantic. If that was not enough, however, the ballads of the singers and guitarist that went from table to table would not disappoint. They knew me here. Not because I had become the dating gigolo of Greenwich Village, but because I was truly enamoured with the place in it's entirety. It was not uncommon for this restaurant to have a Joie referred customer join them, at least once a week. They showed their love, in return, with giving me VIP treatment. I could tell that Denise was as impressed by this as she was with my well pressed suit and crisp white shirt. We drank, ate, held hands and stared into each others eyes. It was very much the perfect date in spite of her ill use of the English language and poor vocabulary. These were my cleavage years. Although my brain would often wince during a less than intelligent conversation, I found solace in a beautiful cleavage and my illicit thoughts.

We held hands, walked and made it to *The Duchess* just as the DJ started and the dance floor opened up in the back.

I was in my glory sitting with her at a table near the dance floor ignoring her uneasiness. I chalked it up to the loud music and stayed focused on her cleavage without her noticing. We had stopped talking for the first time during our date when the salsa started playing. Saved by the rhythm of some great music, I asked her to join me.

Denise could move. She knew turns that I had never seen before. Most remarkable was her ability to make those turns look like my choreography. I was leading a very skilled dancer who was actually leading me in disguise. The music engulfed us.

As much as we danced the night away, enjoyed each others company, laughed and partied, something was amiss. I know that now but I concentrated on the "good time" back then. The city was still very much alive when we left the club at 1:30 in the morning. We decided to walk a bit before saying goodbye. I was working towards a night cap invitation.

She held my arm and squeezed it. "This was a great date." she said, like it was not a full sentence. "But?" I asked. "Nothing, I'm just tired and maybe a little tipsy." "Time to go home." That sentence seemed so final. I was not pushy and I did not intend to invite myself to her place for the night. We had really just met, after all. I did expect that this "great date", as she put it, would segue to date number two. The second date where Tony would join me and we would both explore the depth of that cleavage. I quickly referred to black and white film swagger when I asked "when will I see you again?", as I hailed her a cab. The suit, her dress, the night; it all felt very *James Dean* suave. She didn't answer right away. I opened the taxi door to help her in. She was muttering "I'll call you.", in a rush as she sat down. I started to take money out of my pocket to pay the driver for her ride to Queens but she put her hand out "No, no, no... just go." I know that she could see the hurt and confusion in my eyes. I did not understand what had gone so suddenly wrong. She grabbed the car door to pull it shut, almost on me, when I felt a hand on my shoulder spin me around.

The first punch hurt like hell and made my nose bleed. The second hit totally pissed me off. My crisp and bright white shirt was bloodied. Denise jumped out of the car screaming "Paddy don't!" I realized at that point that she new my assailant but I could not comprehend what was going on.

I loved that shirt. I had picked it up at Saks Fifth Avenue. I decided to fight for my outfit and lunged at the dyke who had just hit me. She stepped back and showed me a knife in her hand. A good old fashioned New York stiletto switchblade. The kind of knife that killed Bernardo in West Side Story. I realized that I did not want to die for my shirt. "What the fuck is going on?" I yelled. I was angry and frustrated at not being able to hit her back.

"She doesn't know about me does she Deedee?" this Paddy person asked her. Denise turned towards me with such sadness and tears in her eyes. "No and I'm so sorry Joie." she said. "Sorry? I should cut you both the fuck up." Paddy yelled and slapped Denise hard. I felt so helpless. Under normal circumstances, I'm a scrapper that is willing to swap punches to defend myself and others, but she had a knife. I concluded that they were a couple as the screaming and slapping went on. A couple that fought hard on the Wednesday that Denise and I met at the bar. A couple that had been together for five years until just this very night when Denise pseudo ended it. She felt abandoned, unappreciated and unloved. I deciphered this all through their shouts and fight on 7th Avenue, at 2:00 in the morning, while still upset about my shirt.

Apparently, Denise had shared our date plans with Paddy just before she left their home to meet me, in a twisted effort to revive their relationship. To make her jealous at my expense. Scarier then that little tidbit of information was that Paddy was stalking and watching us all night. She was drinking Bacardi straight, out of a flask, while massaging her switchblade in her pocket. And all the while watching me wine, dine and dance her lover.

I flagged down another taxi and asked them to both get in and go home to work it out. I was disgusted with Denise and sick of this whole rumble scene they had made me a part of. I needed to go back to the club to wash up and take off my shirt before going home. Denise mouthed that she would call me when Paddy put her head down, balling her eyes out, but we both knew that I would not get nor take that call.

All eyes turned towards me as I walked back into *The Duchess*. They were concerned that I had been mugged. I explained what happened and passed on calling the police. I was embarrassed. Not because I had been hit twice, in the streets no less, but because I felt used. I misread all of the signals of that date completely and felt so stupid.

The coat check girl would tend bar during the spring when that room would remain empty. They kept a first aid kit and some cleaning supplies back there. She invited me to that back room to help me clean up. Unbeknownst to me my top lip was cut and bleeding too. She applied a butterfly stitch and nursed me quite adeptly. "That's a big juicy lip you have now." she was playing with me. I wasn't that swollen. I was pouting, and with my mambo lips, well you get the picture. She was also able to get some of the blood stain out of my shirt. Had I not spent twenty minutes listening to Paddy's hysterical rage, she would have succeeded to get it all out. I took the shirt off to wash it at home and put my suit back on with just an undershirt on underneath, Miami vice style. "You look brand new. How about a drink before we close?" I agreed, mesmerized by her South African accent and gentle touch.

Coat check girl was actually a really beautiful woman. Like magazine gorgeous. I had noticed her many times but knew she was out of my league. I would find out that her name is Sophia. That name clinched the huge gap between us for me. It was so close to the word sophisticated. Still, nothing beat a failure but a try, so I would play the part. "What will you have?" she asked, now back at the bar. I didn't want to order my usual beer and set the wrong impression. "Surprise me. And remember I've been beaten severely." I jested. She smiled and served me my first *Brooklyn*, a delicious cocktail made with rye and maraschino cherry juice. There are a few other things in it but I could not take my focus off of her.

I noticed how much my face hurt when I smiled. I thought about her and the possibilities on my way home to Staten Island in a cab that evening.

Sleep came quickly. I dreamt that I contacted Denise to replace my Saks Fifth Avenue shirt that night.

Golden tide

4

She is like an ocean wave.
That crashes into my every thought.
I can taste her salt on my lips.

She is like a summer breeze.
That envelops my every move.
I can feel her warmth on my hips.

Sophia was the siren of my youth, hailing straight from Greek mythology and luring me to *The Duchess* every night with Tony always in tow. She had it all, at least in my naïve mind; sex appeal, exotically beautiful, an accent and she worked at the bar that I was most frequenting these days. That she had seen me at my worst, beat up and bloodied, was now unimportant. I was smitten. And she was often annoyed.

She was never rude. My tips still paid the rent. Let's be honest, I was not as bad as some of the lounge lizard lesbians hitting on her daily. I was just young and persistent.

I had thrown out my blood stained Saks Fifth Avenue white shirt along with any memory of my date with Denise. I was focused on Sophia, my dream combo nurse and bartender.

It is hard to believe that I am so painfully shy in my natural state when I recall these stories. By this chapter alone, one would think that I was not. The truth is that authenticity is a very powerful force when fuelled by your libido. I also had a healthy ego thanks to my parents. You could label them dysfunctional for many reasons but they did give us a strong sense of self-admiration. I will stumble on to humility face first, chapter by chapter, I assure you.

I carefully satisfied my Mama's craving to be with her first and only Grandson, at the time, to pursue this coquette. The schedule would cover several months and into the winter.

She made every entrance into the club as if she was coming through the curtains of a runway show. Every outfit she wore accentuated her beautiful curves but she never revealed too much skin. She was so out of my world. I lived through the constant reminder and ridicule of my friends. Like a mosquito drawn to the light, I did not care about surviving the experience of her, I needed to have her. Looking back, I know that she toyed with me, and basked in my attention. Sophia had no reason to come to the back part of the club. Both the coat check room and bar itself were right up front when you entered through the door. Still, she would always make the rounds, greeting people before getting to me for a playful hug or kiss on the cheek.

I leaned out of one such hug when I shouldn't have causing her to kiss me on the neck. My knees buckled and I could feel the lipstick souvenir on my skin. "You smell delicious" she would whisper in my ear. Her words were glazed with an accent that often caused me to lose control of my composure followed by the use of my limbs, at least properly. Was Sophia teasing me because she thought I suffered from a neurological disease? I was willing to play the disability game if needed. Surely it was a better explanation for the many times that a beer bottle went flying out of my hand and across the room, instead of being the wave hello that it was intended to be. Or when I would trip and fall into some innocent bystanders' lap as she walked by me. I struggled with depth perception and balance when around Sophia but I longed to show her how well coordinated I was in bed.

I saw nothing wrong with one night encounters that would hone my sexual skills whilst still in this chase. I discovered some new way to bring a woman to climax with each experience. My prosthetic pal was becoming a local hero.

I believe Sophia misunderstood my libido influenced interactions, without her, as a change in interest. Nothing could have been farther from the truth. So I was shocked when she giddily introduced me to 'Car' short for Carmen, a name that did not befit the truck driver standing in front of me and at least a foot below my eye level. The fact that Car had her arm securely around Sophia's waist confused me on so many levels. When did this happen would have been easier to answer than how. "Yeah-howya-doin?" Car would ask, in almost one word, and with the raspy voice of a cigar smoking whiskey drinker. What was happening here? I feigned an urgent need to go to the bathroom and ended our conversation quickly. I smiled and was polite but somehow I knew that Sophia understood. The bathroom was in the basement. There were no windows. I needed to breathe this out. I needed to think. I would leave *the Duchess* early this evening.

If she was out of my league, Sophia and Carmen were from different universes. I was convinced that this mismatch was her ploy to push me away.

I would have to survive many months of their loving on each other in public before I put that theory to rest. Somehow these opposites had become attracted to each other and it was gruesome to watch. Even more disturbing was my creation of their voices together during sex in my head. It was haunting to imagine that beautiful voice and accent calling out any one's name but mine during an orgasm. I would often think about it at work, especially on my club nights. Sophia would get the wrath of my unrequited desire when I would come in.

"Hey Snow White." I said. My greeting and jab combo directed at Carmen's height. She smiled, knowing that I was crazy jealous, and still being respectful of her clientele.

We still had great conversations at the bar. I made her laugh hard and often earned myself a free beer, but the real bonus was always the ever so slight touch and brush of my hand. These began to last longer and longer along with eye locks of such depth that I could see her shudder. My friends questioned my sanity and frankly so did I. We gave what could be my neurosis a name for everyone to be weary of. '*I.I.*', pronounced like a sailor's agreement, stood for infatuation imagination. "You're suffering from some serious *I.I.* Joie." they would say when I told them that we were making love without touching.

Her reaction to Car surprising us at the bar during one of these moments solidified that I was not suffering from '*I.I.*' at all. Sophia stepped back from me so instantaneously that the momentum caused her to hit the bar shelves behind her. She was flushed and nervous like someone hiding a lover under their bed. I turned to look at Carmen, still bewildered by my ability to mind fuck, and recognized the rage on her face. That was the same look that cost me my beautiful white Saks Fifth Avenue shirt more than six months ago. I stood up and stepped away from the bar to allow them some privacy. As much privacy as is possible in a crowded lesbian club in Greenwich Village New York.

I grooved to the music while watching what appeared to be a very tense conversation between them from across the room. There were people all around them and all I could think of was how classless it was for Car to do this at Sophia's place of employment. She had to stand on the bar rail in order to yell in her face, so their fight was obvious to everyone. Sophia would try to walk away to tend to her patrons but Carmen grabbed her wrist. I started to step forward just as she shook herself free and walked away, under the bar door flap and straight to her manager standing by coat check. I saw a tear roll down her face in the nanosecond that she took to look at me, just before leaving through the front door. Carmen would surely chase behind me if I left to join her. I decided it was best to let cooler heads prevail and enjoy my free beer.

My favourite bartender took some vacation time; they would tell me. I joined her, but separately of course. It would be more than two months before we would see each other again. I didn't expect to go out on this cold winter evening after comfortably hibernating all of this time. She was not in the club when I arrived and so I found my way to the back, not expecting to see her at all. I don't think I would have missed her, had she disappeared. I was quite content with what we had even if my friends called it "*severe I.I. bullshit*".

She walked into the club wearing a fur coat over a winter white wrap around dress and stunning high heels. There was a substantial crowd inside, and in between us, but our eyes locked once again. Her hair was flowing beyond her shoulders. You could not decipher where the animal fur ended and her wild hair started. I wanted those high heels on my shoulders.

Sophia walked straight through the crowd right towards me. We kissed so hard, so deeply, wrapped around each other physically and mentally tangled as well. Like a scene out of a movie everything moved in slow motion and I could no longer hear the music. She smelled like the ocean and I was caught in her riptide.

I thought it strange that she would check her coat and come back to me on the dance floor but as it turns out, she was now a patron too. The crassness of her public fight with Carmen was the impetus for her to seek employment elsewhere. As luck would have it, she would receive a response to a job application while brooding at home for these two months. Sophia was now employed at a New York advertising agency taking full advantage of her marketing degree. She was also no longer involved with anyone, or as I teased her, she was 'Car-less'.

I would spend the night waiting on her, for a change, and catching up on all of the times that I wanted to make out with her in the dark corners of the Duchess. I'm sure that we came twice, just kissing. Sophia and I would leave the bar for her place and a night of infinite wetness. It just so happened to be one of the few times that I had left Tony at home in his drawer.

The travel to her apartment, how long it took and where we ended up is a complete blur. I had my hand in her tiny G string and my finger between her lips. She gasped when I found her clit, still struggling to find her keys in her purse. Her fur coat was warm and sexy. I would have fucked her inside the coat, and in the hallway, but she somehow opened the door. We fell inside her apartment when the door opened. Her kisses were desperate.

We stopped long enough for Sophia to be the gracious hostess. I rolled a joint for her while she hung up our coats and brought me a beer. She was drinking red wine. Not having developed my palate for wine yet, I thought that was so sophisticated back then. I smelled the finger that had been inside of her when I licked the joint closed.

My high made me want her more. I wanted to move my mouth from her kiss and down her body, slowly. I wanted to savour every part that I imagined while only privy to her beautiful smile at the bar all of these months. Her high kept me at bay, so that she could talk and explain something that she felt was extremely important.

Sophia went on to explain that she had been physically abused by more than one ex lover. She told me how the argument with Carmen scared her that night and how it immobilized her, both physically and mentally, for many weeks. I listened as intently as someone who had waited for this particular piece of ass for eight months could. We were touching throughout the conversation. I stroked her hair and her cheek. I kissed her eyes when they saddened. But I was irreversibly horny. If I had balls they would be purple by now. "Shhh, I would never hurt you." I whispered. I stuck my tongue in her ear and she moaned. She stood up, took my hand, and led me to her bedroom. The bedside table glowed an amber colour setting the mood. I pulled her close and breathed her in while untying her wrap around dress. She took it off of her shoulders and let it fall to the ground. I removed my button down shirt over my head. I saw the scar on her chest as I gently laid her down. It was definitely not a surgical scar. It was a jagged ugly scar that ran from the tip of her left clavicle bone down, between her breasts, and finally to just above her navel. It was like a child had drawn mountain range on her body. I could only imagine that someone had viciously tried to split her in two. I kissed it from beginning to end stopping only to suck her nipples to the point of her first orgasm.

Her hips moved wildly. She opened my belt and put her hand inside my pants and caressed me. I put two fingers inside of her and slipped my pinky into her ass. We could not stop cumming together. The joint had kicked in completely and there was nothing off limits this night. One position segued into the next, like a stream finding its path. We kissed and smiled and look into each others eyes through the sweat pouring down our faces. This was eight months of pent up desire and our bodies wrapped themselves around each other as if possessed. It was surreal to hear her voice and that accent screaming my name along with Gods.

I finally descended, between her legs, and parted her labia with my tongue. Gently at first, licking until her clitoris swelled for my sucking. I buried my face inside of her. Licking and sucking until I could feel it fully engorged, on the verge of climax and then I slipped my fingers inside of her too, one back in her ass. Sophia's back arched like a convulsion and she shook uncontrollably. Someone in the bowels of the building yelled "shut the fuck up" just before she started to urinate.

I lifted my face up quickly but she got me. I tried to keep my hands inside of her but she would not, could not, stop. I sat up to watch her fully pee on her bed. So much so that it puddled beneath us creating a small piss pool that we were both wading in. I waited for her to stop shuddering and still squirting me, us, on the bed. It seemed to go on forever and the smell eventually repulsed me. It was dripping off of the bed and onto my clothes strewn on her floor. I picked everything up and made my way to the bathroom.

By the time I came back out, as clean and fresh as possible in urine splashed clothing, Sophia was in the kitchen. The pool of piss remained on her bed. I could not imagine how she would clean that up. I did not offer to help. The experience had not just sobered me but I may have been in shock too.

She wore just a t shirt in the kitchen and had not gone to clean up. I said no to a cup of tea or coffee. It was past five in the morning and I needed to pick up my son in four hours. Sophia did not try to explain nor did she apologize. There was no sign of embarrassment whatsoever. It was as if this was the norm for her and I was the only one overwhelmed by it all. I kissed her goodbye, admittedly a rapid and repulsed kiss. I did not ask for her number and she did not offer it. That she was very stoic and expecting me to disappear is the best way to describe what happened. I wish that I could have disappointed her, and moved past it, but I was too young.

I would see Sophia in *the Duchess* many months later in the spring. She was still as beautiful and alluring as I remembered her to be. We greeted each other warmly but no more than that transpired between us. She told me she would never forget me one wine filled night in that club. Ditto. I would forever remember her as the Queen of the Golden Shower.

Butt plug anger

5

Funky, fetished, freaky me.
Yearns to live a fantasy.
More than two I decree.
Her and her and me makes three.

What I'll learn one needs to know.
Not every yearn should be a go.
Unbridled lust, a human flaw.
The lesson is ménage à trois.

Coqui and I are communicating again. He calls me often. As karma would have it, Gigi would dump him for a friend, someone he introduced her to. He made her known to the neighbourhood drug dealer. A Panamanian who had a reputation for violence and excess. Much like a movie depiction, he drove around the 'hood' in a Mercedes Benz cashing in and getting whatever he wanted, including Gigi. They call him '*Toco*', a Spanish word that means touch or play, and he was a dangerous player.

I listened to Coqui's endless explanation of how he and Gigi came to be, followed by how he still loved her, and ending with a semi-decent apology and attempt to be friends again. It seemed so long ago for me now. Not necessarily in time, but in value, or importance to my current life. I did not hold any grudge against him. He was definitely changed by the break-up.

Work with AT&T doubled and tripled for me in the months that followed their break up. I wanted to always be available to listen to him but I was exhausted. The job had also slowed my personal life. The months that followed my night with Sophia were piss poor. Coqui and I made plans to play handball in Brooklyn as soon as I had a free weekend. It was the only way I could stop his nightly calls about nothing.

New Yorkers, and Latinos in general, play handball like no other people. There are plenty of official courts in every borough but every wall is open to use by avid players. Coqui was one of them. He looked at every building with the eye of a spots engineer, assessing walls for the ultimate handball game. We played with an ace ball, a small black rubber ball that stung when you hit it. Handball is a game played with attitude and a lot of trash talking. It is at its center a New York street sport along the lines of stick ball or stoop ball.

We chose to play against the wall of the funeral home on Atlantic Avenue. The side wall was really on Wyona St., in East New York Brooklyn, down the block from where he lived.

The warehouse door entrance next to that wall was where the bodies were brought in. We had so often seen them drop bodies that were too heavy and clumsy on the gurney right onto the pavement. Coqui would always help them lift a body up and into the facility without issue. Then he would rub his hands all over me telling me he was "killing' my game." We had no fear of the dead. It was good to have my buddy back in all his silly and often stupid, obnoxious glory.

We were in the midst of our third game and sixth beer when Gigi strolled up arm in arm with Toco. His aura made us feel uneasy immediately. Toco was an ugly man. Part of that ugliness came from within him. His face was severely pock marked and he had a mouth full of gold caps. In typical thug mode, his neck jewelry weighed more than he did. And he smiled like a snake, lips pulled tight and across his face, with his tongue constantly flittering as if he was tasting the air. I suspect this was a twitch that he could not control. We did not know each other. I only knew of him. These were not my circles other than my getting a joint or two from Coqui that had made its way through the system, managed and owned by Toco.

Coqui was buff and although short in stature, very handsome. He had the café au lait colouring bestowed upon him by his interracial parents, with very light brown, almost golden, eyes. It was the era of mullets and huge afros. My friend had one of the biggest and most well kept *'fros'* in Brooklyn. His hair had blonde highlights.

He was just getting ready to serve when they walked up. Coqui's smile was shy but fully dimpled when he saw Gigi. There she was looking at the both of us, her past, holding on to snake faced Toco. The testosterone was stifling and even I was exuding my own, although a much gentler version.

Gigi came right towards me and kissed me ever so gently on the cheek. We had not seen each other in so long. She was Tony's first vagina, I thought proudly. "How are you Jo?" she asked, ending the question with a beautiful smile. "I'm good." And I was, just not completely comfortable at that moment. Coqui and Toco were starting to circle each other in that way that male animals do around the female of their species. "Que lo tuyo?" (*What's with you? in Spanish*) Toco would ask. He had that Latino hoodlum swagger. At this moment, he looked like a Hyena walking around Coqui. "I'm ready to serve and you're in front of my court." This would have been an insipid response had he not grabbed his crotch and spit on the ground right in front of snake face, which is Brooklyn street sign language for suck my dick. Just as Toco's eyes became slits and he recoiled to strike I yelled "HEY!" taking every one off balance, including Gigi. "We're just playing some handball." I said loudly to no one in particular. "It's good to see you Gigi. And I'm so glad you're happy."

She had not said that at all. As a matter of fact, her body language spoke volumes. Instead, what I saw in her eyes was that she was glad to see me in particular. That she regretted going on to Coqui and that she feared the person she was now with. So much so that she didn't dare leave him. But my saying "she was happy" put that tongue flittering smile back on Toco's face. He walked over to Gigi and took her hand leading her back on their walk to somewhere.

Coqui looked confused and was enraged. I would give him back his manhood by allowing him to beat me in our homemade

Heineken Handball Tournament. Maybe he truly beat me on his own. Those exact details escape me. What I do remember is Gigi looking back and mouthing the words *call me* while Toco's head was turned in another direction.

"She smiled at me Joie. Did you see that shit? Right in front of her man too. Haha. I know she misses me. Fuuuckkk, she smelled so good too. The girl is fine but the girl is trouble." Coqui would go on and on, wide eyed and chirping, but no truer words had ever come out of his mouth.

He called me constantly. At first he needed to rehash the handball incident over and over again. Coqui was convinced that Gigi wanted him back. He conjured up stories of saving her from the evil snake face. A lot of his conversation was under the influence of marijuana. He found good work as a security guard at a construction site. The job paid well but was boring. Some of the benefits included that he could smoke a little pot in the booth that he was in all night, alone, from nine pm to six am. I was attending my AT&T classes and memorizing cable colour patterns and connections, according to those colours, to install data circuits at the stock exchanges in New York. They were moving away from teletype to modern modem driven networks along with monitor stations and printers. I was the first female hired and a part of what would become New York history. I needed to pay attention and study.

Most times I could tolerate his crazy calls. He was, after all, such a simple man and good friend. It broke my heart when he told me he had a seizure on the job. Coqui underwent several tests following that seizure and in multiple hospitals before he was finally diagnosed with epilepsy. His conversations changed. The prescription made him loopy and he was told not to drink, or anything else, when he took his meds. With no outlet, a boring job, and embarrassed by his disease Coqui's calls were often dark. He had persuaded himself that Gigi was coming back to him and he spent a lot of time at home waiting for her, and calling me.

I was shocked when the phone rang and I picked it up to her voice. I fully expected it to be Coqui telling me why life wasn't worth living and me spending an hour or more convincing him otherwise, or making him laugh. "Surprise!" she said with that sexy dangerous voice. She had spun me for a loop before. The voice at the other end of the line was now Toco's girlfriend. I was very much aware of that situation. "Well, well Bonnie, does Clyde know you're calling Tony's handler?" She laughed hard. Did I mention the power in her laugh? Mesmerizing comes to mind and I struggled to not be drawn in.

We spoke for almost an hour. I would find out that which she wanted me to know. I agreed not to ask questions about Toco, their life, and most baffling why him. I slipped and called him snake face and she threatened to end the call. I acquiesced only because she was telling me about not being sexually satisfied. She had my attention, still, after all of this time.

The conversation grew raunchier with every word. We did not give it a name back then. Calling it phone sex would have ruined the moment for us. Without reference to what was happening, we merely felt each other's every word, every description until it drove us to touch ourselves during the call. Gigi and I came together, again, for the first time in almost a year. It was not enough. We had released feelings and wants that she, at least, had been stifling for a long time. She teased me with the expertise of someone who had been experimenting for a lot longer than I had. I became even more engaged when the topic of a threesome came up. Gigi, according to her, had had several and was quite fond of them. It would not have taken much to convince me in my current state of mind but she took extra care to describe the gloriousness of three women in one bed together. She introduced me to the words ménage a trois. What could be more satisfying and erotic than those words. Words that phonetically opened your mouth to speak them so perfectly. I agreed to be the top to her double bottom sandwich. She had a friend, she said. I had Tony, I countered. We hung up our call knowing that I would need a babysitter out of my home next weekend. I would describe it as an intense study weekend to my family, friends and especially Coqui. I would not let any thought of how she would get away from Toco take space in my head. The one thing on my mind involved three.

I was impatient with almost everyone during the week before my first threesome but especially so with Coqui. The timing of his calls, let alone his conversations, were always awkward. I did not share my weekend plans with him, of course. Instead, I tried to mediate his internal battle to confront Gigi with his love for her and even more frightening, his plan to square up against Toco, once and for all. This particular train of thought was just bullshit spawned and achieved by his drinking a Colt 45 beer, 40 ounces, along with his epilepsy medication.

The sad truth is that the week before Coqui had experienced a seizure on his way to buy his '40' on a night off from work. He had been strolling along listening to his beloved salsa on his newly purchased boom box when it happened. In those days, the bigger the music box, the more you flexed your muscles carrying it. He took his leisurely walk in the hood wearing the standard and tight white t shirt, along with sharply pressed jeans, and flaunting his perfect fro. Every muscle rippled as he ditty bopped his way to the local bodega. He would go on to tell me that he was moving and grooving to the rhythm of Ruben Blades big hit *Pedro Navaja,* playing on cassette, when he felt the aura that "smelled like shit." He knew the seizure was upon him but did not have time to take himself out of harms way.

I would visit Coqui in the hospital the day after. Toco and his boys watched Coqui hit the ground hard. His nose would be broken upon impact with the cement sidewalk. They ran over in what appeared to be an attempt to help but instead the bastards stood around him and laughed. He could hear them laugh even through his body twisting into a painful and longer than normal episode. It was a Grand mal seizure. They fought with his contracted muscles for that newly purchased boom box, held in his tightly closed hand, and beat him severely until they knocked him unconscious out of the seizure and his body released. They finished this act of pure cruelty by clearing him of any cash he was carrying, before urinating on him. He told me that the smell was in his nose for weeks. "The mother fuckers pissed on me Joie." he would often reminisce sadly.

Two of the five boys who attacked him would be caught and go to trial but Toco was never implicated. Everyone knew he was one of the perpetrators, including Gigi, but he had a reputation for closing mouths.

Coqui healed, at least physically, and went back to work once again saving up for the boom box of his dreams. His head would never be clear of the embarrassment and fear, especially since it made the local paper when the two thugs were caught. I tried to tell him that they were cowards and street slime, that did not deserve time in his head, but he started every call telling me of his mental misery.

Saturday came like a flash. Gigi and I spoke the evening before to confirm our big date. I dropped off my son Corey to his ever so excited grandmother and spent the better part of the day cleaning. I had created a vision in my mind where multiple partners meant utilizing multiple spaces at my place. A ménage a trois playground. Just to be sure I attacked the apartment cleaning as if I would be placing an ass on every surface. When the time came to shower and get dressed, I destroyed my closet before settling on sweats and a muscle shirt. How does one dress for imminent undressing? The sweats would drop quickly, I thought. The muscle shirt looked great when half dressed, just in case a frenzy ensued. I checked the fridge for beers, assessed the liquor situation and then practiced my door opening and greeting for maximum *suave*. Tony was placed right in the middle of the bed along with a variety of condoms and a butt plug. I was brave until the door bell rang and I threw a pillow on top of it all.

Gigi walked in like the majestic drug lord goddess that she had become. She was 'ghetto-licious' and in such a short amount of time. My eyes set on *'Party in my Pants'* contestant number two. Her name was Dina, short for a much longer Latina name. I would find out exactly what that was after smoking our first joint together but promised to never tell. She was pretty in comparison to Gigi's gorgeous but she seemed much sexier. Dina was smart sexy, if that makes sense. I realized immediately that she was well read, well spoken, and classy. I considered her my gift for the evening and could not wait to unwrap her.

Coqui called just as we were laughing it up and getting comfortable with each other. I had a spherical couch at the time. Completely round, much like a papasan chair, only big enough to hold five or six people. I laid in between Gigi and Dina as we passed a joint around and shared our cocktails. We were comparing belly buttons when the telephone rang. "Shh shh." I giggled, and said, in an attempt to quiet the ladies so I could answer what rang like a desperate call. I knew it was him. I also knew he was persistent and would venture over if left ignored.

I tried to sound studious and "not high" when I answered. "Hello?" "Yo J, it's me. I am going out of my fucking mind again. I need to tell Gigi that I love her and get her away from Toco. You have to help me. And I need to seriously kick his Pan am ass or he will kill us." His words were slurred and clearly he had not thought this out. "Coqui I'm studying." I said to muffled snickers and an 'Oh shit.' from Gigi or Dina. "What was that? he asked with a tinge of hurt in his voice. "Who you studying? You got company?" followed by his nervous laugh. I worried that he would recognize the laughs and voice in my background. I answered angrily. "I'm not studying 'who' fucker. That's the TV I'm studying cables and telephone lines. And I can't talk right now. I'll call you later." I had turned my back on the women at that point. They could hear me. "Alright, alright." "But don't forget to call me Jo." he begged in that little boy voice. We ended the conversation with "Love you creep." And "Love you back.", as was our normal. I made a mental note to call him in the wee hours of the morning when my adventure was over. I turned around to find both women naked from the waist up and playing with each others breasts.

    I dove in between them and put my lips around Gigi's nipple. I knew what she liked and how to make her wet. Dina leaned in to stick her tongue in my ear and put her hand down my pants. Her perfume was sweet. I took my mouth off of Jegana's breast to kiss Dina while my fingers played in Gigi's panties. Dina tasted like rum and she smelled like coconut. She was my living, breathing and undulating Pina Colada. Gigi bit my neck. She always liked it rough but there was an incredible savagery in our wanting each other. I needed someone's pussy in my mouth. The pot, the liquor and my Latin libido kicked in on high. I grabbed them both by their belts at the buckle and zipper of their pants and lifted them up to follow me to my bed. We put our three mouths, lips, tongues and wants together as we walked to the bed and collectively collapsed on top of it. I made a mental note of where Tony and the accoutrements were positioned around us. The three-way kiss was hot and full lipped luscious. What was left of our clothes on was ripped off like a factory mechanism with many hands. In an instant, we were completely naked. I positioned Gigi's legs up and behind her head and went down on her while Dina and I slipped our fingers into each other. Her cumming in my mouth was swift. Her juices were thick and sweet. I could not get enough of drinking her in. Dina pulled at me and writhed in my hand. She was holding my wrist and humping my fingers desperately. I was three deep when I reached over to where the sex toys were located and found the butt plug first. I slipped it under my chin and into Gigi's ass as she pushed herself harder onto my face. Her groan sent shivers down my spine. I managed to find Tony in strap next. Through the power of my pain numbing high and incredible agility, I slipped my legs through the strap and positioned Tony, without losing tongue or finger rhythm with either woman. Dina was desperate to cum. I had been toying with her. I scissored us together so that I could slip my nine-inch cock inside of her while now playing with Gigi with my hand. The bed began to move back and forth with all of our movement. *Sukuki, Sukuki, Sukuki*...the sounds of our fucking and the smells of our collective juices filled the air.

Dina began to scream my name as she started to climax. She moved her head around my arm and pulled me away from Gigi. We were face to face and making out with Dina sitting on Tony on my lap. The strap was pulled tight on my clit and I could feel every pull backward and every push forward. We moved faster and our tempo answered every throb. The world around us blurred. I held my orgasm, several orgasms, to be able to explode together. Every kiss and every thrust became primordial. She placed her hands over her eyes and arched her back away from me before calling for God and announcing her cum. I held her waist as this happened and put my tongue in her navel. When I finally let go it was to fuck her as deep as I could, pulling Tony back until I could just see the head peeking through her labia, before going deep again. Not just in and out, but with the hip movement of a seasoned Salsa dancer. That cum lasted what felt like fifteen minutes straight. Dina's juices pooled in my lap along with my own. She came forward and kissed me gently on the lips and we laughed, shaking from the seismic magnitude of our orgasm together. And we hugged. That kind of *oh my God* hug when you find someone that you have been looking for for all of your life. She looked amazing with both her cleavage and thick thighs covered in sweat. Her skin glistened gold.

I turned my head to see Gigi ripping the butt plug out of her own ass and looking at us as if we had run over her puppy. I pushed Dina off of me and scrambled to restart with with Gigi, as she was getting out of the bed. I was sweaty and sticky and had left my 'mojo smoothness' mixed with Dina's wet puddle on the bed. I tried to kiss her neck and get her going again but I was clumsy and we both knew I was faking it. Apparently, and for the record, if you have to apologize to any one person in a threesome than it was not a successful threesome. Although I begged for forgiveness, Gigi felt slighted and I suspect also embarrassed. There was no going back. She had witnessed me have something with Dina that she and I had never had, on top of my abandoning her in bed. Dina was also flustered by what had happened. We both felt something when we looked into each others eyes, at the very moment when our hearts beat as one; something beyond the sex.

We would never try to explore what could have been between us. She was a true friend to Gigi and I also held on to some semblance of loyalty to Toco's girl. The greatness of our orgasm would be overshadowed by the sadness of how the night ended. It was almost four in the morning when we all slowly dressed, with as little conversation between us as is possible. I offered a meal, coffee, tea and all that a polite adult would offer at the end of a visit. They both declined. Gigi gave me the hug of someone who could smell Dina all over me. Dina gave me the hug of someone who would miss me.

Toco and Gigi married a few years later after having a couple of children. She would have five in total when he was finally arrested for trafficking, murder and a variety of felonies. We spoke a handful of times after he went to jail. It was always because she needed something or because she wanted to borrow money. I gave her an antique Timex watch that I had inherited from my Mamabuela when she passed, during one such meeting, in my weakness, and because she spoke about going back to school and working. She seemed genuinely appreciative of such an emotional gift. My Mamabuela would have done the same thing. I suspect that she pawned it at some point in her life, like anything of value that came to her ownership, for Toco's perpetual appeals and legal debt. He would never see the light of day again and Gigi aged much too rapidly. She remained ghetto long after she lost her 'liciousness'.

I would run into Dina in nightclubs throughout the years. She stayed bright, classy and as sweet as her coconut perfume smelled back on our special day. Always smiling and friendly, no matter who she was with, she had the uncanny ability of always making me feel special, while keeping me at a healthy distance. A distance whereby we would not talk about that night again for fear of remembering how wonderful it was. It was part of an unspoken commitment to our friendship with Gigi. Every once in a while our eyes would meet and she would take my breath away. There would always be an unspoken 'wow' between us.

Homage to a frog

6

Your departure did not make the news.
Your life was not remembered.
In so many ways you paid your dues.
But kindness never rendered.

A man who did not shy the word.
A voice that needed to be heard.
I close your story with words within.
Let all who read this know my friend.

The ringing startled me out of a deep twelve-hour sleep. I could smell stale vagina and rum on my pillow. I pushed the dirty butt plug away from the telephone, disgusted, as I picked up the receiver. Instantly, I remembered that I had not called Coqui back and so I braced myself for his whining.

Hearing his sisters voice on the other end of this call did not make sense. It entered my ear like a foreign object, like a q-tip pushed too far. I felt pain in my fog. "Coqui is dead." she said. I don't even remember that statement following a proper hello. My mind had parsed out that which was not as important as why she was specifically calling. There was no care in how she delivered the news. It was flung at me with the same momentum in which she had received it. I managed to ask "how" in between gasping for air. "He killed himself." she would answer, so matter of fact. There was no net to this free fall of information.

Naidy would go on to tell me that Coqui had been found in his security booth on the job, Sunday morning. He had fashioned a noose over the door and hung himself using telephone cable available at the construction site. The irony of these details were not lost on me. The stabbing pain in my chest was intensified by every bit. The rest of the conversation was choppy. "You okay?" "Yes." "You?" "Don't know." "He's gone?" "Sure?" "Yes." "Oh God!" We both cried into the telephone at each other. She promised to get back to me with the funeral information.

My head was spinning and my son would be brought back to me in less than hour. I called Mama right away and faked my really bad flu symptoms. The crying and hang over made my lie easy to perpetrate. "Are you in pain?" she asked innocently. "Yes Mama, I am in so much pain." I was able to say without hesitation.

She counselled me in how to take care of myself. She also vehemently refused to bring Corey home, no matter how much I said I would be okay.

That evening I put everything that was about our friendship in bed with me. My worn handball glove with the fingers missing. He had thrown these at me one bright summer day just before a game. "This should help improve your control creep." he would say. I also had a box full of Ace black balls. We would take turns supplying our games. There was a myriad of Salsa mixes on cassette with his handwriting detailing each recording. We shared a love for Latin music although Coqui did not dance. I thought I had plenty of time to teach him. The hair pick and scarf he had left in my apartment for his always perfect fro. I watched the art to that coif so many times. He would pick his hair out as big as possible then gently place a silk scarf over it for that impeccable round effect. He would spray it shiny afterward. "Like a dance floor mirror ball." I would tell him when he asked how he looked. And all of our pictures together. There were countless pictures of us laughing and hugging. I never noticed how many until he was gone. I never noticed what a significant part of my life Coqui was until his passing.

We had grown together, not grown up together. Coqui and I traveled out of our teenage years and into adulthood together. I met him when I started dating his sister, during a time that I was still dating boys. He hated me for my indecisiveness back then, because it involved her. As my relationship with Naidy waned to just a friendship, he and I grew closer. It had nothing to do with compatibility. Coqui and I were very different people, with different upbringing, from different parts of New York and varying likes and or dislikes. We grew close because we genuinely cared about each other, and unconditionally so.

We laid on the front hood of my car, on a blanket, sharing a joint and a beer. The stars at Riis park beach at night were brighter than ever. If you didn't know any better, you would mistake Coqui and I out on a date. Nothing could be farther from reality. These were the occasions when he would encourage me to be me, with what would be interpreted as strictly male thoughts to anyone else in that day and age. And, as straight as he was, this was a safe place for a man from the tough streets of East New York Brooklyn to express his more feminine thoughts too. Our haven, our mutual reassurance and respect, often allowed for very deep conversations about life and pains. I would forever miss these confessions and discussions. "You know I hate my real name." he once confided. "Alberto? Yeah that's a pretty fucked up hick name." I jested. "Not because of that." he would go on after a snicker. "I hate it because I'm Alberto Jr., after my father, and he beats my Mama senseless sometimes." I don't ever want to love somebody like that." he would finish. "Dang Coqui. I'm sorry man." "You feel like an ass for calling me a hick now, don't you." he said with a smile while putting the unlit end of the joint in my ear. We would always end these sometimes tear and snot filled talks with guffaws.

Coqui and his siblings grew up as part of an interracial family when it could not have been easy for them. His father was a black man of Jamaican decent and his mother, a blonde blued eyed woman from Puerto Rico. She had older children, his step siblings, who were also very white. They were very unkind to their brown brother and two sisters. It was hard for me to grasp such prejudice existing in their own home and such horrible treatment and violence amongst brothers and sisters, however it paled in comparison to how his father treated them all. His mother was a cold hearted woman who defended their father's actions, including her own beatings by him. She was crazy too.

She once asked me to pull my pants down and prove that I was a woman, on one of my visits to pick up Naidy for a date. I froze in their living room, not knowing what to say and embarrassed, until my date came downstairs and saved me. I was nanoseconds away from pulling my zipper down to drop my pants and expose myself to this person, their Mother. They all grew, barely out of high school, to move out of that house. They did so easily and without help. Like being let out of a prison.

The Coqui is a tiny frog endemic to the Caribbean, most of which are located on the island of Puerto Rico. It has a much longer and scientific genus classification, however the locals call it Coqui, mimicking the sound of its mating chirp. Anyone who has been on the island can attest to the symphony of these tiny creatures' voices, once the sun sets. It is very rare to actually see the frogs but it is often said that they demand to be heard.

Such was the reason for his nickname. Alberto Jr. witnessed unimaginable violence and very little love, if any, in his house. I never saw his parents happy and I certainly never saw them show affection towards any of their children. I will not use this chapter to write of their "dirty laundry" or give them more ink than they deserve, but suffice it to say that my friend demanded to be heard as an adult. I don't know who gave him the name for his incessant talking but I would thank that person today if I could. He never felt the pride of being Alberto Jr. but he shone bright as Coqui, always speaking his mind and bearing his heart.

I don't willingly attend funerals. My family has guilted me into going to the few that I have attended. When you grow up watching your frail Grandmother take on a spirit and start speaking like a man, possessed at a viewing, you tend to shy away from them. I had taken to mourning and the paying of my respects in my own home, where I could cry and reminisce comfortably. That said, I wanted to go to Coqui's funeral but his family prohibit me from doing so. Naidy told me it was because they were embarrassed by how cheaply they had gone with all of the arrangements but I convinced myself that they knew everything I was feeling guilty about, and that they despised me for it, as much as I was hating myself. I drowned my sorrows in Colt 45 beer in honour of my friend and to numb all that was plaguing me about his death. That I had had a threesome with the woman that he loved. I wished that I could have told him that it was a complete failure for her and I. And that I could have shared what happened between Dina and I. He would have called it love right away and pushed me to pursue it. I felt terrible about lying to him about who was in my apartment. Most of all, my pain was about speaking to him angrily and promising to call him back. I'm so sorry Coqui.

Over the years, and on many non-sober occasions in my life, I have contemplated the events surrounding Coqui's death. I now know that there were deeper pains to cause him to want to leave this planet than I could have inflicted over night or during our friendship. I stopped crying every time I had to work with telephone cable and forgave him for using it to take his life. While it was in poor taste, and I still bear the scar, it is just possible that it was in ode to me or simply a coincidence with no forethought whatsoever. He is missed and I still hear him. You made the book Coqui. Salud!

Clit Club Candy

7

Hot flesh, unsatisfied
Enough I've cried
Let me soak in your sweat
So that I may forget
A guilt so brutal

Fascinated with your dance
The trance, inviting
Bodies uniting
My libido keeping time

I managed to go on with my life, like many do after losing someone significant. The daily routine of being a mother, a daughter, and working, eventually took over. I knew that I was finally mentally present when I recognized that the butt plug of threesome night fame was still dirty. As I set out to sterilize my toys, and Tony, I also awakened my sex drive. My friends had been calling me for weeks with both condolences and ideas of how to regroup. I agreed to go to my first strip club. This adventure made sense on so many levels but most of all it was a fitting goodbye to Coqui.

The *'Clit Club'*, as we called it, must have been a meticulously cared for, but illegal establishment. I could smell vagina once we were past the security entrance; two large bouncers placed between two doorways, known as a mantrap. These behemoth greeters were authorized to ask questions, request identification and finally frisk or scan you for any weapons or drugs. The smell was not rank or dirty in any way but instead inviting, almost floral, like the warm and naked body of a woman. The entrance cost beyond security was twenty dollars. That was considered steep in those days but the *Clit Club* was known to be well worth the cost. Thursdays was ladies' night only, so there would be no boner driven assholes to deal with, just those of us that are "prosthetically" inclined.

The woman at the door, past security, was thick and unusually pale. I suspect that she did not see much sunlight in here, in addition to be one of the whitest women in New York. "It's her first time!" my friends managed to harmonize giddily as I nervously scrambled for a twenty-dollar bill amongst a wad of strip club singles. "Welcome to the stable virgin Mary." She replied in a very Southern accent. She smiled as our eyes met. They were the colour of the ocean, turquoise, and she had the most stunning long eye lashes. If eyes are the window to your soul hers seemed to be full of pain in spite of their physical beauty. Her face told a story of disappointment. Wherever she hailed from, I know that she did not come to New York with the dream of checking people in to a strip club in lower Manhattan. She held my hand and stamped it with bright purple lips.

I would enter this establishment with the same feeling of awe and wonder that I remember entering Disney World with as a child. The stage was shaped like a five-point star in the middle of a very large space. Each rounded star point had a pole on it. The chairs surrounding each star point were comfortable and high backed like thrones. The club was plush and every customer was treated like royalty. It was, after all, a traditional gentlemen's club with all of the vagina smelling grandeur.

The bar surrounded the room on all four sides. I would come to know how important it is to be able to order a drink quickly, immediately upon the first five dancers coming to stage in front of their respective poles. The MC for the evening stood in the center of the star. He introduced each gorgeous creature by their stage name, as each was spotlighted in front of their pole. He described each of their kinky talents so clearly and in so much depth, it was like an audio delivered porn movie. We all wriggled in our seats.

I sat right at the tip of one of the star points in the front row of four, a place of honour for a strip club virgin. The minute the light shone on Miss Candy Cane she picked her head up and our eyes locked. I kept reminding myself that it was her charge to get as many dollars from the new kid as possible. I froze, amazed by her beauty and flexibility. Just as I was sure that an uncontrollable drool would roll over my mambo bottom lip and into my drink, I was elbowed from both sides and in unison. "She's going to move onto somebody else if you don't pay her for that feeling you're having right now Joie," my friends insisted. Somehow I knew she would not but their voices released me from the strip club trance state that she had put me in. She was on all fours now. I rolled a couple of dollars up into a straw shaped payment and placed it in my mouth for her to retrieve. I saw an ever so slight smile as she came off of the stage, to the rhythm of the music, and put her hands on my knees. Candy Cane walked up my legs, with her hands, leaving her feet on the stage. She took the money from my mouth with hers and delicately transferred it under her bra strap, like the pro she was. Then she leaned in and kissed my lips lightly, and winked, before using only her core and thigh muscles to raise herself completely back on stage. It was magical! We spent the rest of the night engaged in this crazy strip club competition. I wanted to be the most unique giver of money and she surprised me with taking it from me without ever using her hands. Unbeknownst to me the joy of this evening would not end here. My favourite people in the world of that time had also arranged for me to have a lap dance by Candy.

The lap dance studio, as it was called, was a separate room partitioned into approximately ten private areas, by curtains only. Bouncers stood outside of the velvet curtained lap rooms, able to hear and help the dancers immediately, should anything go wrong. Inside each of the lap rooms there was a love seat and music delivered to both you and the dancer through individual headphones. She would pick the music.

I was so nervous that I was visibly shaking. The savvy club management would take this waiting time to offer expensive shots with very sexy names. They also sold cigarettes, cigars and poppers which were legal back in the day. Poppers is a slang term given to alkyl nitrites that some people inhaled for recreational purposes, especially in preparation for sex. I opted for a pack of Newport, smooth menthol cigarettes, that were my weakness at the time. I also had 3 shots called *'Sit on my face'* before Candy walked in. I was vibrating up until that point. Candy was petite, all of 5'2", with a voice to match. Her body was ripped, clearly from her dancing acrobatics. She was sexy in every which way, but it was her smile that I was immediately drawn too. The deepest dimples accentuated her perfect pearly whites and thick heart shaped lips. She was there to rub her body all over me and yet I was imagining that which I would not get with this lap dance, a kiss.

She entered the room with a tray that held a cassette, what I thought to be poppers but turned out to be essential oils, and a drink for me. It was obvious by her actions that she was very professional about the process. Candy never said more than *"Are you ready?"* in the first 60 seconds of prep time. Watching her added to the excitement and anticipation. It also relieved my shakes. She placed my set of headphones over my ears before putting hers on. I did not notice the ottoman and tables in the space until she lifted my legs to make me comfortable and place my drink on the side table. 'Let me be the one' by Exposé began to play in my ears, to my disappointment. I was hoping for something with a more primal fucking kind of beat for my first lap dance. How naive I was, now that I think back, to believe that a lap dance has anything to do with sex, or more precisely my satisfaction. If you're spending money on them to this end, then I am here to tell you that you're wasting cash. I don't know for sure but you Can probably solicit full on sex for less money.

You barely touch, if at all. The laws did not allow for full body contact during this time. There is a space between both bodies that is veil thin, with a great dancer. It is designed to arouse your mind and to teach one control. Candy Cane knew her art well. She mind fucked me for forty-five minutes straight. It was transcendental. We became part of the music both individually and together. We breathed each other in and when she licked her lips just barely centimetres away from mine, every hair on my body stood on end. She smelled like lavender and at several times during her dance over me, her eye lashes touched me.

The music continued past the initial tune by Exposé throughout the entire dance. It never transitioned into thumping humping music but instead into a lap dancing mix that highlighted her incredible sensuality. I felt it coming to an end and put my hand on her waist, her skin, without thought. I instantly panicked, not so much afraid of the bouncers dragging me out to the embarrassment of my friends, but because these were her rules and I didn't want to offend her. Candy jumped but did not recoil nor did she remove my hand. We kissed. It wasn't a make out session. I understood that all could be heard. It was just a gentle exchange of our tongues. She put her pointer finger to her mouth telling me to be quiet about it, quietly. She whispered her every day name in my ear and asked me to hang around. For that instant, I thought, the woman who barely touched me has touched me very deeply. I was smitten and so I waited.

My friends vacillated between this being a huge mistake and my being their sheroe. I struggled with the entire concept of being interested in a pole dancer. It was cliché in the worst of ways but I could still smell her lavender on my lips.

Candy looked much different under full lighting and in her street clothes. She was still very cute, don't get me wrong, just different. I will never know if she was sexy because of her profession or in spite of it. My posse, her name for my friends, moved themselves to the bar when she walked over to formally introduce herself. I learned that her name was Linda, but never stopped calling her Candy. It fit. She was so sweet. She sat down beside me with two more shots. "The bartender told me this is your favourite shot," she said as she put another *'Sit on my face'* in front of me. I was embarrassed but managed a reflex reply.

"It's my signature move and drink." It sounded just as lounge lizard then as it does here. Candy smiled the way someone does when they know you're nervous and put her warm hand on top of mine. "You don't have to try so hard. We are not going home together tonight. But there is something about you that I like." She went on to write her telephone number on a hard card board coaster that was on our table. "I'm exhausted." She said right before downing the shot. "Call me and don't be corny when you do." She stood up and leaned in to kiss me goodbye. "I can't promise that." I stood up quickly to say. "Promise what?" she asked. "That I will not be corny. I come from a long line of Taino natives. We perfected corny and by the way, also corn crops." I was nervous and my reaction is to be funny or die. She laughed hard. "Okay, so maybe I should have said don't be crazy. I meet a lot of crazies in this business." I was still enjoying the moment of her laugh before replying but the truth is that I could not promise that either. She walked away towards the door when one of the bouncers joined her for the walk outside. Just before reaching the door she turned around and yelled back at me. "What's your Taino name so I know who is calling me?" "Joie." I replied and we both laughed. I shoved the round coaster in my pocket excited about tomorrow and calling Candy.

I spent hours and hours on the telephone speaking to Candy. She was a Pace University student majoring in computer science and quite the programmer, aside from pole dancing. She was smart and sweet and while we often slipped into dirty talk, it was her mind that captured my attention on these calls. Our first date was to walk along Nassau St. in lower Manhattan before heading to the South Street Seaport for a meal. She would be getting out of a lab class and this was all near her school.

It was the perfect setting for my awkwardness and goofy side to emerge. I tripped on the cobblestone streets every other sentence, unable to speak and adjust to the Un-level path at the same time. "Are you drunk?" she asked, half convinced. "No, I'm entertaining." I answered. I purchased three oranges from a street vendor just to juggle them and prove my sobriety and coordination. Candy laughed hysterically as a crowd encircled me in typical New York fashion. Her smile and laugh made me forget how we met, for that instance, but it lingered back there somewhere where it mattered.

Dinner was fabulous at Fluties, a restaurant owned by football great Doug Flutie. I kept calling it Floozies, as in promiscuous women, in an immature attempt to be funny. She winced but never skipped a beat at being the adult she was. Conversation flowed easily and so did the drinks. By the time we left the seaport we could not keep our hands off of each other. I went home with Candy that night.

Her place was like a library. There were books everywhere. And not harlequin novels but heavy, heady, and thick writings about Nietzsche, Nostradamus, Edgar Casey, C-Language and Kinesiology to name of few. We threw them all on the floor as we wildly undressed each other, trying to find a spot where I could devour her.

She was even more tiny naked. And muscular. I lifted her up into my arms and pushed her back against the wall. She climbed me and put her legs over my shoulders, putting her wet pussy completely in my face. I dove in for a very long time and we ended up in multiple positions and in multiple places that first night together. It was daylight when we finally stopped to eat and sleep, 36 hours later.

Candy was due at the *Clit Club* that night. It was Wednesday night and fully a gentlemen's club for the evening. We could not stop kissing and discussing the books around us in between naps and meals. When it came time for her to get ready the conversation became very serious. "I don't want to let you go," she cried. "Why can't I go with you? I'll just sit in a corner at the bar. I'll take this book called *Man Alone with Himself*." I joked and begged. "You do your thing and I'll be alone with my book." I continued. Candy giggled and put my face in her hands. "Can you promise to remember that my dancing is a job and not me?" I nodded yes. "No matter what you see tonight?" she added. "What will I see?" "If you have to ask then you can't come with me." The conversation went back and forth like this for almost an hour before she agreed that we would go together. The debate turned us both on and we went from a cuddling talking position to a full on fist fuck that made her cry when she climaxed.

The taxi ride to the Clit Club was playful. We were both in a giddy state of sexual euphoria. She held my hand and kissed me often during the drive but the minute we pulled in front of the club, she let go. Candy became a stripper and pole dancer as soon as she entered through the back door. She whispered something to the thick pale door woman, who proceeded to lead me to a spot at the bar. There was no goodbye or I'll see you later. She went from warm and loving to *I don't know you* kind of cold. "My name is Cara." I was acknowledged by the door girl. "Hey, aren't you the virgin?" "Yes. "I replied meekly but whispered "Not anymore." under my breath. "Alright, well order anything you want for a total of three drinks or less." she barked at me. "This is on CC's tab." she yelled to the bartender while pointing at me.

I felt alone, and so young, as a parade of men in their late fifties or older made their way into the Clit Club. The bile made its way to my throat just as the MC said her name and the light shone down on her.

Unlike my virginal night at the club our eyes did not meet once. Candy teased and seduced every man in her section much like she did me. They were vulgar, animals, who touched themselves into visible erections. The behemoth bouncers were kept busy. Many patrons were escorted out for holding and inappropriate touching, or grabbing. Her face was blank, no smile and truly no sign of being there, like a very flexible mannequin. I took it personally. The night felt long and I grew tired of watching her work her magic. She was truly the best of the club. It took me all three of my allowed drinks to do so, but I finally sneaked out when she went on to the lap dance room. I left her a less than sober note that read: *I loved our date and time together. I'll call you tomorrow. Had to leave. Can't stomach the whore you.*

Candy didn't answer my calls for several weeks after that night. I eventually had to make it back to the Clit Club, around closing time, to apologize to her. Both Cara and the behemoth bouncers were on alert when I showed up. I was sincere. "I may be too immature to handle this properly but I want to see you again and I am sorry." I started. "I am not a whore." Was her only response. She was in tears. "I know, I know. I was stupid and drinking vodka. Have I told you that vodka turns me into a mean Russian." I could see the bouncers move closer as I leaned in to hug her. She cried hard in my arms that night. Not because of my note, I would find out, but because she hoped that I would be different from the many others who had said and done the same or worse.

We left the club to go to her place and this time we talked more and made love. Strangely enough, sex was not constant with Candy and I, as it is for most new couples. She worked in the sex industry and was horny for her mind and soul to be touched instead. I spent a lot of time studying with her, both her courses and my AT&T path training. A couple of joints smoked

71

often turned into a deep Talmud debate. She was brilliant but I still struggled with her chosen, although temporary, profession.

It was our only argument or disagreement. In the eight months of our dating, and being together, I had had over ten altercations in the parking lot, just picking her up. I could not understand the ownership that many of these psychos felt for her. Thank goodness for 'Wall' and 'Mountain' as I began to affectionately call the bouncers. They would sometimes drive us all the way to her home to make sure no one had followed us. It stifled our relationship tremendously. I could not introduce her to family for fear of someone recognizing her or because it might put them in jeopardy. Ours was a beautiful but clandestine relationship until she could get out of the pole business.

That she came home with almost $5,000 a week, also made it a serious decision. She owned her own home, paid for everything in cash including her university education, took care of her parents and was saving to start her own healthcare data management company upon graduation. All fully funded by shaking what the lord had blessed her with at the Clit Club. As much and as often as the psychos showed up in our lives, these creature comforts would sedate us in between arguments.

It was another Thursday ladies' night that I decided would be benign enough for me to be in the club so that I could go home with Candy. Everyone knew me and that we were a couple now. I no longer had a three drink minimum but nobody would ever serve me vodka, not that I dared bring out the angry Russian again. I came with flowers and I was enthralled by her excitement over them and her attention. She kissed me several times before going into stripper trance. The place was unusually packed with women, mostly couples, and the occasional more masculine older dyke. The women were not psychotically aggressive and they didn't touch themselves into a sticky state either. I could handle the adoration and gifts, especially money, from this crowd. I was okay with the lap dances on this particular night too. This had become the only night that I could tolerate being there through the show and not just picking her up. I had brought my study material too.

When the night was over, and Candy met me at the bar, she was visibly exhausted. It had been a packed night, ending in six lap dances, after her vigorous nightly performance. I knew taking her home would mean just cuddling and sleeping tonight. Tony would remain in my bag unused tonight. Perhaps I could talk her into a quickie, standing up, of which she was a master at.

I was deep in this thought as we approached the street with Wall and Mountain about ten feet behind us. A man in a black hoodie pounced on us out of the blackness of the street, on her side, and grabbed at Candy. Before I or the bouncers could move towards him, he shook her hard and pulled her in his direction. They wrestled him easily and flattened him to the ground before calling the police, but not before he broke Candy's clavicle leaving her writhing in pain on the side walk. He was 6 foot 4 and muscular. He had also been carrying a box cutter. As horrible as it was to follow her into the ambulance and hear her cries as they stabilized her arm, the police assured us that we were very lucky. I spent the night with her at St. Vincent's' Hospital Emergency Room and we went home to my place afterwards. Although she pressed charges, there was concern that he could be released within 24 hours and that he may know where she lived. We were living the stripper, television cop show, nightmare.

She would be incapacitated for nine months following the attack but would face a lifetime of panic attacks. The injury, not to mention phobias as a result of the attack, changed Candy's life dramatically. Several ligaments and shoulder muscle tears left her unable to ever pole dance again. The medical costs cleared her savings and she eventually sold her beautiful home in Queens and went back to living with family. We tried really hard to maintain a relationship but her fears got the best of her and I was too young to be patient. She very rarely ventured out past 5:00pm. She did stay in school and graduated with a degree in computer science. Her degree landed her a great position with Metropolitan life, last we spoke.

The court case went on for sixteen months and Rafael Espinosa was sentenced to three to five years for stalking, assault, and some other intentions that were discovered when they searched his car and home. He murdered a stripper / dancer two months after his two-year release for good behaviour and may have died in prison by now.

Candy and I still "hooked" up for many months' even after we stopped dating or trying to maintain a relationship. "We're so sexually compatible." she would often explain, mostly to herself. It got old and weird and I eventually drifted with the goal of losing touch.

We ran into each other many years later and I was happy to be introduced to her lover. I was happy for her. We hugged hard and I said. "It's so good to see you Candy." "Please call me Linda." She replied.

Uptown Girl

8

Tortured soul.
Asshole.
Both need help.
We all need love.

I vowed to never step foot inside a strip club again following Candy's attack, and our little relationship. I have kept to my word as of the writing of this book. I was still in love with Manhattan; dark streets, bright lights and all. My work kept me there and all of the best clubs were in New York city. I would mimic the Mafioso style of life, with my family in Staten Island and my playground in the city that never sleeps.

For a period of time, in my youth, that slogan took on a new meaning. Cocaine kept the city busy and it was everywhere. In the deep dark underbelly of the island, it could be purchased cheaply. And amongst the affluent and chic, it was available by the bowl full.

My work took me to what is now known as Tribeca, technically the *triangle below canal* street. It was fast becoming the home to many Wall Street stars who were building enormous condominiums and living in grand apartments there. One such was Simon, name changed to avoid a law suit. They had dispatched me to install his direct access to both the New York and American stock exchange systems, a privilege that is bestowed to very few, even with todays sophisticated encryption and cyber security. He was busy when I arrived, multitasking on both the telephone and on the computer. Simon had the energy that one would expect of a broker. He was fast moving and fast speaking, while gracious, but somewhat impatient.

The apartment was magnificent if you imagined no one living there but instead existing in that space. It was monochromatic, lots of leather and stainless steel. The view from his work space, which should have been a dining room area for us "little people", was over looking the water and simply breathtaking. Every step, every sniff and all movement echoed in

Simon's apartment. Today, I would find that space cold and uncomfortable but back then I was in awe of it all.

I remained professional and connected the equipment that would access the various networks that he would have entrance to. The installation process involved my also making connections in the basement of this building, out to the world, and to the risers that led to his specific apartment. It was involved and a very careful course of action that would also have to be tested through and through. I would have to insure, as an AT&T engineer, that the circuit was not only secure but also redlined. This meant that in an outage, this particular circuit would take precedence and either remain up and running, or be one of the first to be repaired. Redlined circuits very rarely go out of service. They are routed on protected paths that are both resilient and redundant. The President of the United States communications network is redlined. I would do the same for Simon, over the course of a two-day installation.

By the time I finished turning up Simon's direct access to the world economy I knew he was exceptionally well off and high most of the time. His pacing, his sniffing, his jaw movement and his moments of incoherency were exhausting, to be quite honest. I needed to teach him how to login securely, use the system and display exchange activity on his many monitors as part of the acceptance process but his concentration was terrible. He would call AT&T to extend the time allotted for this acceptance period with me, at a premium cost of course. It would take two weeks past the two days of installation. He wanted me to be his friend after this technology binding experience. I was not allowed to accept gratuities in any form, and doing so was cause for dismissal, but what I did on my own time was my business. I accepted an invite to his next chic party providing he understood that I was a lesbian. "This isn't a freaky and kinky rich man orgy kind of a party?" I asked. "No." he said, entertained by my lack of social graces. "There will be lots of famous people, some of who are lesbian too." "I want to introduce them to my tech genius who made all of this possible." I really had built an exchange monitoring center for him. It was one of my finest accomplishments for AT&T. He baited me with both the compliment and the promise of mingling with a higher class of people. I would spend the next week finding something to wear, for just such an occasion, at Saks Fifth Avenue.

Simon answered the door flying higher than I ever saw him before. He wore a beautiful gold coloured, raw silk shirt, embroidered with red Chinese symbols but it stuck to his sweaty man boobs like white on rice. He hugged me like we were pals and announced me to everyone as HIS engineer. He paid AT&T over fifteen thousand dollars for my extended time and the installation. I suppose he was right about my being HIS.

Someone put a glass of champagne in my hand while another came out of the darkness to pass me a joint. The entire adventure was becoming more and more surreal by the minute. I walked around, really seeing his apartment for the first time. The art on the wall was locked down, museum style, indicative of its value. I was astonished looking at what appeared to be a genuine Picasso when George walked up to the painting beside me. "Are you thinking about how to remove it from the wall without notice too?" he asked. I recognized the Latino Cuban accent right away. "No, I'm wondering if it is a real fucking Picasso." I answered. George laughed and introduced himself properly, hand shake and all. "You're his engineer and I am his cocaine dealer." he said. I did not flinch because I did not care. Nor was it a surprise. I heard many cryptic one sided calls to George during the two weeks plus two days that my office was relocated to this apartment. He stared at me with the slight smile of someone trying to figure me out. George reached into his suit jacket pocket and offered me a small brown glass bottle of powder that I could only assume were part of his wares. "No thank you." I said as I moved on to the Tomato Soup can Warhol on Simon's wall." He followed me. We would go on to discuss Simon's amazing art collection, reviewing each piece as if we were in a gallery. "So, you don't do coke?" he would ask as we stared. "No." I explained. "I have a bad heart valve." "I don't do caffeine either." "That is very rare and admirable." Said the cocaine dealer. "Thank you." seemed in order.

Diana sashayed over and put her long arm around Georges shoulder. She was so tall and big boned I mistakenly took her for a beautiful drag queen. I could not have been so wrong. Diana was a fashion designer's assistant, or as she would put it, the slave girl behind the curtain. George introduced her as his beautiful wife. "This one is cute, Papi." she said to him while rubbing my shoulder and fixing my lapel. "I think I make her nervous." Her laugh was loud. She was loud. And it echoed in Simons apartment. "She is interesting too, Nena." He would go on with an accent. "She doesn't do coke." He said it as if he didn't believe it or as if I was his challenge. "Oh my goodness, she's a Unicorn." Diana could not speak without touching me or hanging on to me. "Do you fuck?" she would ask. They both laughed. "Are you here with a boyfriend?" She looked around for someone nearby me. They reminded me a bit of Morticia and Gomez Addams. "No" I snickered. "I'm a lesbian." "I like that." she answered, now smelling me. Diana was stoned out of her mind. What started out as touching was now full on leaning. George realized I was holding his wife up now. "It might be time that I take you home, Nena." He would say to her. "Aye si, take me home, Papi. This party is boring." She would say much too loudly, again. Diana leaned in to kiss George, off balance, and slobbered his forehead. "Okay, let's go home." He would start to direct her out. "Wait, give the unicorn our telephone number. I like her." "And uni, come here." I would walk over dreading that she would touch my hair. "You see that skinny bitch over there. She likes women too. Go have fun." She would push me in the direction of the woman with great force and that loud laugh. "The truth is that I can use an engineer too Joie." "Please call me." George would hand me his number as he escorted Diana out of the apartment clumsily. She was so much bigger than him. As strange as they both were, they were very entertaining. Who was the "skinny bitch"? She looked familiar.

Gia Carangi frequented all of the parties and clubs in the early 80s'. She was always accompanied by someone she was obviously trying to get away from, an agency watch dog cramping her style. She was breathtakingly beautiful, and yes a bitch, both of which were enticing. Her tortured soul shown through from across the room.

Two hours into Simon's party and I was now bored. The lavish 6000 square foot apartment had been darkened for the event, the perfect lighting for a den of iniquity. Everyone was stoned, wealthy or fake. Some were all three. I sat on the couch to compose myself and contrive an early way out and alone. The white leather couch was so supple it swallowed me up upon impact pulling her towards me. She was intoxicated and laid her head on my shoulder. In an apartment with bowls of cocaine on several glass tables throughout, Gia was clearly doing something else. Another drug, along with another drink, had one of Americas' top fashion models practically in my lap. Her hand slipped down into my lap and she grabbed my thigh in her long fingers and squeezed it tight.

Gia had great pouty lips, even more so in her current state, and they were on my shoulder for the taking. I turned my head and gently brushed my own against them. She smelled like pure moonshine. She squeezed my thigh even tighter and slipped her hand up to my crotch. I'm sure her vital signs were minimal but she proved the point that lust is the last thing to go with her response. I took the chance, and a taste, by slipping my tongue in between her lips to part them. She came in tighter and put her thick tongue in my mouth. Gia grunted and groaned like a bad porn actress while kissing me. Her kiss was sloppy and became forceful. I grew uncomfortable with her pinning me down on the couch. The harder she pushed the deeper she embedded me in its plush and supple folds. Everyone around us was stoned as it was, so what appeared to be a hot and heavy make out session, was actually me fighting to get away from her. Lust had turned to panic. My eyes were open staring at her. I was worried that she would bite my tongue. She had such a strong sucking hold on it, that it hurt where it was connected to the inside of my mouth. I finally slipped my hands between us and pushed hard against her shoulders. A shove so desperate that I knocked her off of my lap and onto the floor, in one fell swoop. I stood up ready to hit her when Simon came running over and put his hand on my shoulder. Several people helped her stand up, barely. She was incoherent but aggressive. I checked my lips and mouth for blood and dusted myself off. Gia was clearly upset but her speech was severely impaired. I took a good look at her and realized that this beautiful model was actually quite butch. I felt violated and disgusted. Simon apologized profusely. She was well known for her antics, I gathered. Her watchdogs whisked her away into the darkness of the huge apartment.

Simon had someone bring me a rum and coke. He went on to tell me how she was a top model but hooked on some bad drugs. He joked about how I could someday brag about making out with Gia Carangi. I never understood calling someone an asshole as much as I did at that moment.

Cocaine Engineer

9

All that you acquire.
On the backs of sad addiction.
High society gets higher.
While you practice dereliction.

Hypocrites galore.
Tend this fancy ass drug store.
And while the dealer counts his dough.
Someone's life went up their nose.

I reached out to George and Diana once my head had cleared of what had transpired at Simons gathering. They remained entertaining and introduced me to a new life to say the least. I eventually dabbled in a line or two, but I had seen too many lives destroyed by this drug to do more than that. I was also privy to George and Diana's lavish lifestyle paid at the expense of many. Although he had a plan for the white picket fence house and children with Diana, George would never achieve his goal of getting out of the drug business, at least not voluntarily. Sadly, I would witness his dreams go up in smoke.

George explained his quandary during one of our many walks and talks. He was quite the civilized gentleman and it was often unbelievable to me that he was a big time cocaine dealer. It was all managed very business like and with a very careful upper echelon clientele. Diana, on the other hand, was a dealer's wife and user straight out of a bad movie. She was not just loud but obnoxious, a heavy drinker and had began doing Georges coke too. She loved me, her unicorn as she affectionately called me, and I would become her husbands prize engineer too.

The dilemma with selling cocaine was insuring its purity percentage straight to the buyer. Seller A would make a deal with buyer D through broker B who was actually in the mix thanks to C. Each would take their cut, both monetarily and in product. By the time it was in D's hands it could be half as great as when it left A's. The chemical cure for this, back then, was to cut the almost 90 percent pure cocaine with a highly numbing but less expensive mix. Coke users associated the numb with grade A quality. The problem, Georges issue, was that once it was cut it would become powdery. Another attractive feature for serious buyers was that it be in rock like form as is pure or close to pure cocaine. George asked me if I had any ideas for turning powdery, and cut cocaine, back into rock form. He stirred my creative juices by telling me just how much such an invention would mean to him, in US dollars. My only request was that I not have to be in his "drug facility" to work on this or test this. My ex husband, Corey's father, had been in the wrong place and at the wrong time when he was killed. We agreed that I would come back to his apartment, which was drug free, when I had completed my thoughts and design.

I fashioned a metal frame made from iron table legs. It was fifteen by fifteen inches square and I had each joint and corner welded for extra strength. I also purchased six inches of iron pipe, a screw on fitted cap for one end of the pipe, an iron disc that fit perfectly into the pipe and portable hydraulic jack whose saddle would fit smoothly into the pipe and against the iron disc.

I practiced with household powders that would not generally stick unless there was enough pressure to push what few moist molecules were in the powder into a clump. After several approaches, I finally demonstrated it for George in his own kitchen. I lined the six-inch piece of pipe with parchment paper. After placing the screw on fitted cap on one end, I filled it with corn starch, and folded the parchment paper over the powder on the open end. I then slipped the iron disc on top of that and placed it over the saddle of the hydraulic jack. Both pieces, together, would be inserted within the iron welded frame. With maybe three inches of gap between the screw topped pipe and the frame, I would turn the jack on until the pressure pushed it all together within the frame. The trick was to keep it on and between the frame for at least an hour. When we finally released the jack, slipped out the disc and the powder within the parchment paper, the pressure had created a pipe shaped rock. Dropped naturally onto a table it broke into rock like pieces of varying size, that looked just like pure cocaine! George was ecstatic. He gave me a thousand dollars for the idea plus parts and promised me fifteen hundred more when he would try it out with real product.

It worked perfectly and I increased Georges margin by forty percent. I called it *La Prensa*, the Spanish word for press because that's what my mechanics professor would have called it. George would go on to pay me the fifteen hundred dollars promised plus fifteen hundred dollars each time it was used, providing I made three more. This amounted to three thousand dollars a month plus my working salary.

Simons' parties became the norm for me. Diana and George treated me like family. I was their genius, their unicorn, completely cocaine free but responsible for some of the biggest drug deals in the city. They were also benefiting from my simple invention. You could tell money was flowing in that home by George's suits and Diana's high. The more they made the more she took for herself. She also drank too much. And it all was a recipe for dangerous flirting.

I met Renee at one of Simons glorious gatherings. He was South American and an art dealer. He was also a George customer but the vibes between them both was different. Diana thought Renee was gorgeous. She shared that opinion with George more often than she should have. It didn't help that they flirted heavily when high and in the vicinity of each other. "Talk to me about your technical shit Uni." George would say to me at one of these soirees. He was seething watching them and Diana was over the top drunk, or high, or both. Her dressed showed way too much cleavage too. The tension in the air was thicker than those cocaine rocks being created with my *Prensa* invention. I knew something was going to blow and prepared to leave just as Renee rushed to catch me at the door. "Uni." He said. "I understand you're an engineer?" he asked. "I am, why?" "I am opening up a multi million-dollar facility. A gallery. I would love to talk to you about a way to move the art, mechanically and electronically throughout the place, without having to take it down, and for easier storage." I set a date to discuss the details on the telephone with him and said "we can take it from there."

For the next couple of months', I found my way back to *the Duchess* on weekends and spending more time with Corey at home. The *"Prensa"* money was flowing but the tension between George and Diana was just too much to deal with.

George called me to tell me that they were over. He met me in the village for a drink at a neutral pub and poured his heart out. He suspected her of cheating. His deepest sadness he said "I want to have a normal life and family with her." They had had a terrible fight and in typical Latin fashion it declined to ugly and cruel. I remained neutral and offered to mediate although he wanted me to side solely with him. I hate to admit it but I alluded to it only because of my next *Prensa* payment.

Diana called me that night when I got home. Her story was shockingly different. She was in a hotel in Brooklyn. I could not tell George. She was completely sober. Diana spoke of a very violent man who had beat her terribly. She held her own. She was big made woman, as I mentioned, but she was sure he wanted to kill her. She said she always flirted, but had never cheated, and only did so because he encouraged it. It was the only way he could get an erection; to imagine her with someone else. "Even sometimes you Uni." she would go on to shock me. "I'm bored in that apartment. He doesn't let me out, if he isn't with me." "Of course I drink and get high. What else is there?" It all made sense to me, both of them. I did not know what to believe. I told her too, that I would remain neutral. She cried, and finally called me by my real name. "Thank you." she said.

George started to blow his own coke and was a very different man. He lost his classiness. There were little signs of what Diana had described. A short temper in front of me. More foul language. He was just different.

Let's call it a 'divine premonition' but I awoke one morning not wanting anything to do with the *Prensa* business. I called George to tell him. He was very understanding. I felt relieved. It was good while it lasted however I was more excited about my work with Renee. We had exchanged drawings and my design specs. I scheduled time to discuss the details with Renee and his people. We were looking at a six figure design sale not to mention the installation and maintenance contract. Renee was going to introduce me to the people at Sotheby's international too.

George and Diana were speaking again although not together and neither one of them trusted the other. Diana called me to invite me to a party on the Upper West side. They were clients of George who adored her. He had told her he would not attend but felt most comfortable if I joined her. She told me Ashford and Simpson would be the entertainment. I asked if I could bring someone and invited Naidy along. We had not seen each other since shortly after Coqui's passing when she joined me at home to celebrate his life. Naidy and I were still good friends.

George called me just before we left for the party. He was flying high and clearly agitated. He was going to be in the park right across the street from this brownstone. He rambled on and on about how he just wanted to protect her but he was not going to suffocate her. Naidy's neck hair stood on end when she met George in the park with me. "That guy is twisted." She would say. He hugged me and offered us both cocaine, knowing that I would not take any. He said "listen Uni. I am right here if you ladies run into trouble." He pointed to a knife, in its sheath, and stuffed in his boot under his jeans. "I got you." he said with a wink and jaw twitch.

We arrived at the party to no Ashford and Simpson in sight but the music was fantastic. The brownstone was multi level and gorgeous. It was packed with people of every colour and orientation. Servers walked around and brought us cocktails at the door. Everyone was dancing and many people were just humping each other right out in the open. I found Diana across the room and through the crowd. She was loud but the party was louder. As she made her way through I saw Renee holding her hand and walking behind her. His presence shocked me and I questioned their relationship, and how he was here. While I was going to remain neutral, I also didn't want to appear to be part of some lie to George. He was not in his right mind this evening and right across the street. When I told Diana, she went pale, although both she and Renee attributed their being together to a small world, and nothing else.

Naidy asked me to dance and I let go of the drama through several amazing DJ mixes until Diana came running over in a panic. "Uni, I was dancing with Renee and I saw George looking through the window." Naidy looked at me and said "Let's just go home. This shit is freaky." I agreed.

Renee offered to go outside and talk to George. I led Diana and Naidy through the crowd to the basement level of the brownstone. They had propped the door up, leading outside, for added air flow. We thought we heard screams outside just as we reached that door. A calm looking man was looking down at us from the street. Diana asked if we could come out this way. He nodded yes. In single file with Diana first, me in the middle and Naidy in the rear, we ascended the narrow staircase. Just as Diana reached the top, George came flying down the opening on top of her. We all fell to the ground and I yelled to Naidy to run. She ran back in the way we came downstairs. It looked like George was punching Diana. She was screaming "No Papi please don't hurt me, please don't hurt me." I started to move towards her to help when George and my eyes met. I had never seen this man before. I knew it was George but his face was demonic. He came towards me with the same knife he had shown me in his boot. I heard the voice loud and clear. It echoed like Diana's voice in Simons apartment "Run Joie. Turn your back and run. I will protect you." And I did. My feet did not touch the ground. The entire party was spilling out into the street and I ran right into Naidy's arms almost two blocks away. The cop cars had surrounded a four block radius. I didn't understand what was all going on but clearly I, no we, were in the middle of a huge crime scene.

Here is what happened on that upper west side party evening. Diana did indeed see George in the window. He became enraged at seeing her with Renee. His blood tests revealed he had enough cocaine, barbiturates and liquor in his system to kill a man twice his size. George stabbed seventeen people on this evening, killing two. He even stabbed the poor guy selling Puerto Rican ices known as *Piragua* on the corner. He had threatened the man standing over the basement exit to nod when someone was coming up. He stabbed Diana four times. She survived. He stabbed Renee to death and killed a young man that tried to help him.

Naidy and I would ride with Diana to the hospital. Her wounds were not deep. Her begging must have helped but such was not the case for many innocent people. It was a blood bath at Roosevelt Hospital in Manhattan and all caused by one man. I became the translator for the many Spanish speaking victims waiting to be seen in the emergency room. The Piragua man did not want to give them an additional blood sample. "I'm bleeding like a stuck pig. How much more do they need?" he would say and ask in Spanish. He had been stabbed twice in his ice shaving arm. "They can take the blood from my shirt." His biggest concern was his Piragua cart and that this mayhem had cost him a night of business. I felt for him and fought for him in English. When it came time for him to sign his treatment paper he scribbled an X with his non-writing hand. The nurse thought that he didn't understand and asked me to translate what was required. "That's my damn signature. I don't know how to write and that's it." The Piragua man would receive thirty-seven stitches before I put him in a cab to go home.

Stupidly, Diana refused to charge him. She said there were enough people doing so, and the deaths alone would put him away for a lifetime. And so they did. He was sentenced with 25 years to life.

The police questioned me that evening and I denied knowing him, although I gave an explicit account of events as I knew them. It was not a lie. I did not know the man who looked at me in that basement.

I don't know whose voice I heard that evening. I could not decipher if it was male or female nor did it sound familiar. I am simply grateful for hearing it so loudly, even with my deaf ear.

Had enough yet?

10

There will come a time in every life when even the strongest amongst us will break. It may be a tiny microscopic crack or it may seem like an irreparable abyss.

But it is only the mind that is permeable. Our souls withstand lifetimes of lessons towards only one purpose.

That we may learn how to love unconditionally and that we may learn to accept love, even from ourselves.

The next twenty years of my life were a blur like microwaved minute rice. I was not high nor drunk, at least not often. There is no thread or story of addiction to explain all that happened but I still feel it was an abnormal amount of drama and trauma in one life.

I suppose everyone has a portion of their lives where you build upon your intestinal fortitude and really document the lessons. If you didn't need therapy because of your childhood, this is the segment of your being that you need to talk to someone about. I could have become a cat lady or serial killer after these years had I not been severely allergic to either one.

Naidy and I stayed very close after the stabbings. We didn't date in the intimate sense of the word. She and I had put that history away. We were way past that now and served each other as sounding boards through what I can only assume was PTSD. She had always experimented with much more serious drugs, including the injectable type, and I believe that this prevented her from going off of the deep end. I, on the contrary, worked and spent a lot of time with my growing son.

We were partying at The Duchess one night when she announced her enlistment. She had passed her physical and all of her tests and was officially joining the United States Army on the following Monday. Although I was shocked, I never saw her more excited about regimentation and the new disciplined life ahead of her. Which is why I was so surprised to get a call from her saying she was back home shortly after she completed boot camp.

She was undergoing the normal slew of blood tests as part of her physical exams prior to deployment when they discovered something was wrong. She was diagnosed with Aids and medically discharged, all in less than 24 hours. The shaming, and having her dream pulled from under her so swiftly, weakened her in every way. Naidy passed away in less than a year of being diagnosed.

Every one was afraid of this new blood borne virus, but I was intimately involved. My son Corey was diagnosed with Hemophilia. It is a genetic blood disorder and I am a carrier. It is passed down to sons of mothers whose fathers are hemophiliacs. Yes, Aqua man, better known as Papa, had left us many gifts. Some more difficult to carry than others. Suffice it to say that blood was important in my household. Growing boys that are hemophiliacs bleed into their joints as they grow. Emerging adult teeth become a blood bath. Sports, even modified, and physical activity as a whole usually ends in a trip to the hospital where these boys can be given clotting factor, via infusion, to clot and heal from simple injuries that the average child would never notice. It was the hemophiliac community that was first devastated by the aids virus. No one would have ever reacted, or I dare say noticed, had it just been the gay community.

Naidy and I would speak about this ugly virus that was consuming her life at a rapid rate at every visit together. She handled the whole affair like a champion and a wannabe biologist or doctor. In the few short months of her life, after discharge, Naidy compiled a comprehensive journal of what she believed was the American military conspiracy responsible for the aids virus. She spoke of unexplained vaccinations ordered by her superiors. She listed dates and times of when they were lined up, late at night, and given shots that no one dared question.

These were fresh out of boot camp soldiers who had just been trained to obey orders or face consequences. Naidy also spoke of the minorities being separated on just such occasions, receiving what she thought were different drugs based on the side effects that she had also listed. We argued, read and referenced all of her data like two rabbis discussing the Talmud and ancient script. I always went back to her dabbling in intravenous drug use but her argument was strong. She received an intense physical examination upon enlistment. This included many blood tests. They were not just looking for medical issues that prevented her from becoming a soldier, but also any signs of drug use. For one, and her strongest rebuttal, she could not detoxify goofballs out of her system. She was clean upon enlisting, remained clean throughout the process and stayed clean during boot camp.

The aids virus killed people quickly back in the 80s. The medical profession had not discovered a remedy for slowing it down or keeping it dormant, as they have today. I believe much of that progress was hijacked by arguments on how it was contracted and hateful gay bashing. I also came to believe Naidy's theory. Before she withered away, still fighting for her conspiracy theory to be heard, Naidy helped me to see the importance of keeping Corey safe from New York's blood supply of that time. I found incredible doctors to treat him throughout the years with synthetic blood clotting factors, and blood from safe or known donors, rather than the traditional blood bank process. It is because of Lynaida, her full and beautiful name, that my son is one of the few and lucky hemophiliacs who survived that time.

Just to really bring this blessing home on paper let me explain this; Corey was part of a hemophiliac support group at Maimonides Hospital in Brooklyn, New York. It was not just the best care for these boys in all of the state, but dead center to the Orthodox Jewish community, which has very high statistics of hemophilia amongst them. This is a genetic disease that I have read originated with Russian royalty and spread throughout the world as royal families married to create empires through procreative collaborations. My pride in the possibility that my lineage or history may include some crowns and castles was diluted, long ago, with every trip to the hospital carrying my bleeding baby through the doors. It was a difficult condition to deal with during this time, as you can imagine, especially for Corey. The support group made him feel less alone. Synthetic clotting factor cost double and triple the amount of direct blood factor. I was one of the privileged few who came to understand the importance of it, thanks to Naidy, but who could also afford it. Throughout the two years after Naidy's death I watched these young innocent hemophiliac boys, that were part of Corey's support group and his friends, die of aids. None of them were older than twelve. It was a group of thirty-four boys and their families. Many were Hasidic, so there were religious doctrines that prevented them from the synthetic clotting factor that was pig based. Many were Hispanic without the means. Corey is the only surviving hemophiliac of that support group at Maimonides Hospital, of that time. He had angels, I'm sure of it, one of which was my high school friend Lynaida.

In her typical brash Brooklyn street fashion Naidy also expressed concern for my love life, or lack there of George's killing and stabbing spree. "This is not a time to be fucking and sucking anything in a skirt or with a pretty ass Joie." she advised. "Sex will kill you now! And don't believe it will only kill Gay men either. We are all figuring our lives out and there is a long fuck list on everybody's resume."

She said this long before the doctors and media spoke about sex history. It made absolute sense to me and she scared me. It was this fear that had me concede to her match making from her hospital bed, in addition to all of those deep conversations about the military. Before she died Naidy would also introduce me to Mary.

If the term brick house has made it to the dictionary it should include a picture of Mary right next to it. No body of flesh is more akin to that description. She was not exceptionally beautiful and she was of average intelligence. Mary hailed from the Bronx and her attitude reflected that. Never afraid to speak her mind or give up being ladylike to get physical, Mary could go ghetto faster than anyone I have ever known. I disregarded that all because Naidy introduced us, for one, and because of that incredible body that she flaunted perfectly.

It was a time of short skirts, tight dresses and high heels. Mary was all that and a bag of chips on her shoulder to boot when we met. We were both careful and polite. Naidy had introduced us by telephone, set this all up, but passed away before seeing the results. Neither of us wanted to disrespect the dead. My normal quick wit was affected by the cloud hanging over this date so I was not my normal self. I think Mary was not expecting this skinny Mambo lipped and egotistical person standing in front of her. Although we never discussed that first date, or Naidy's description, I'm sure I was over marketed and that I under delivered. We were polite to each other throughout the evening. I took Mary to Tio Pepes not because I wanted to impress her but honestly the choice did not require any creativity. They knew me there and they helped to entertain my dates when my conversation or charm was lacking. She was impressed and it wasn't too long before my swooning skills awakened. The guitarist circled our table to play '*Historia de un Amor*' which translates to Love Story in English. The lighting, the music, the drinks and her enormous breasts guided us that evening. I worked my way past her tough exterior until she finally relaxed around me and actually looked like she was enjoying herself.

Mary confessed that she had a headache and I offered to smoke a little refer with her. I was not a pot head but I imbibed. I expected to be nervous on this date arranged by someone in the afterlife. Don't judge me. I brought a joint with me just in case. We smoked, we laughed, we walked the city, and just before we descended the steps to our respective subway rides home, we kissed. She was from the Bronx and she did not care what people walking around us, to the subway, would think about our making out feverishly at the top of the stairs. The kiss left us both flustered and wet. She whispered for me to come home with her in my ear, with her arms around my neck. She smelled amazing. I was high and turned on. She had breasts and booty to die for and I followed her like a puppy.

The station was crowded and we had to walk single file with me walking behind her. I had not been to the Bronx outside of Yankee Stadium, at that time, and so I trusted that she knew her way home. I prepared for a long ride home from the village but did not anticipate the ever winding and long walk underground. I kept the jokes going as we walked and tried to stay side by side as much as possible. I may have been higher than her and my goofy kicked in too. When we finally stopped walking we were at what seemed the farthest point in the station, on the farthest point of the platform, beyond the stairs and with no one around.

She turned around to face me and stared at me with an evil look that I had not seen all night. "Why are we all the way over here?" I asked. I was not a fan of the New York subway system as it was and was baffled by why we were in the most desolate area of the train station. "I brought you here so I could kill you." she said.

When I finally came to I had my hands around her neck and had pinned her to the station wall. The bright white tile behind her head gave me an instant headache. I was sweating profusely and let go of her just in time to vomit on the platform. Mary's attempt at comedy was as poor as her timing. She did not know about the most recent incident with George or that losing Naidy left me alone to deal with it. We scared each other profusely that evening. I took the long train ride to her place to explain it all. She apologized at what felt like every stop along the number 4 train line to 149 Street and the Grand Concourse. I would find out that she carried with a box cutter for protection so she could have very easily slit my throat that evening, if she really wanted to. It was a tumultuous start to a relationship. I would later find out that it was a huge blood red flag for me to have heeded.

Mary was bisexual. I would not have cared before my year of long discussions with Naidy, and or the aids outbreak, but free love was no more. We cleaned up for a night of talking and cuddling at her place but I was acutely aware of Tony and his merry condoms in my knapsack.

There is something exciting about kissing someone who just threatened to kill you on a desolate New York city subway platform. She swallowed me up with sloppy, passionate kisses that the heart didn't care for but that the groin enjoyed immensely. We covered every inch of her couch in our make out session before she took my hand and walked me into her boudoir.

Her bedroom looked like something out of whorehouse nightmare. There were red tasseled scarves over candelabra lighting. A king sized four post bed dominated the space. The bedding and drapery was overwhelming. She was flamboyant although I did not know this word at the time. She pulled me onto the bed with the mastery of someone who had done this often. We would go on to make out and dry hump each other for hours. If I had to give it a name it would have been "eight play" because we had long exceeded foreplay for sure. I stopped us from going any further as soon as clothes started to be removed. I grabbed my back pack and introduced Tony. She was shocked at my brazenness to have brought him on our date but her wetness told me she was ready for him, for us.

I put a condom on for both cleanliness and lubrication. Somehow a condom makes you feel less guilty about using the same toy with different women too.

I climbed on top of her and Mary's thick body enveloped me completely. Her eyes rolled back when I penetrated her. We fucked for hours to hot salsa music playing in the background. The windows were open and the streets of the Bronx harmonized with the music, my moans and her screams. Ambulances, gun shots and cat screams; we were crazy wild in bed. We stopped when we finally collapsed in unison.

I woke up to Mary's loud voice while speaking to a friend on the phone. "She is so cute and would you believe she had a huge dildo in her backpack?" "La cabrona was prepared honey." "She fucked me hard. I'm bow legged, no shit, but I am getting myself some more of that today…um hmm" I walked out to find her laughing and drinking coffee on the couch, while she spoke.

I had gone ghetto and my ego was enjoying the ride. Say what you will about the crassness of g-licious women but they make you feel like masters of your universe. This Bronx brick house was my biggest fan. She bragged about me to all of her friends and held my arm in public like I was a celebrity. We did not need to have conversations. She was not interested in my brain, nor books, documentaries, travel or even foreign languages outside of Spanglish. Mary was all about our sex life, looking good and going out. Life with her was light and easy in the beginning. I saved all of my brain power for work and my son Corey. She was an endorphin boost. I did not expect substance, so I was never disappointed. I wined her and dined her like any mobster would have taken care of their arm candy.

The other side of what appeared to be the perfect relationship to my former immature self was her explosive jealousy. Mary could not stand any feminine woman looking at me or talking to me for too long. She had a pubic hair thin and short fuse. Even her own friends were subject to her wrath. And she had no qualms about embarrassing me in public. Our hot steamy ghetto sex turned into hot steamy ghetto warfare. The physical fights were often dangerous and vicious.

Two years into our volatile relationship and we still slapped or hit each other without any consideration or remorse. I kept Mary away from my family and my son as much as possible. I had made it clear that I had never fallen in love with her but we continued to have wild uncensored sex, sometimes even angry sex. She was in love, or so she thought, and often spoke about death being the only end to our relationship. Life with Mary became dark enough for me to consider that a viable option for her.

The commercialism of Valentine's day conquered my better judgement. I found myself in a jewelry store buying an expensive bauble for a woman that I didn't love or even like.

Perhaps it was as a result of too many punches and telephone handsets to my head, but I truly believed my ridiculous idea would normalize us. I would present her with this ring on Valentines Day however I would ask that she only accept it if we could be a kinder and gentler couple. I still did not know what falling in love felt like but there were parts of our relationship that seemed to match what my parents had. We would need to commit to anger management together. And the ultimate plan would be to live together.

The ring was beautiful. It was covered in diamonds and garnets. Mary was also a Capricorn and very fond of our birth stone. I had keys to her apartment and arrived there before her just so that I could set the romantic mood. The flowers, candles and music were all in place. *'Always and forever, each moment with you...'*

Mary arrived home at almost midnight. The candles had burned out and I had thrown the record onto 149th street three hours prior to her arrival. She had clearly been out with someone else on this lovers' holiday. I should have been grateful to the universe, and bowed out gracefully, but my ego was riding bareback. She was surprised by my effort, and justifiably so; I had told her that I didn't love her so many times.

She was embarrassed and sheepish to begin with. I was infuriated and volatile. We both knew we were going to have a wicked battle this night but were too young and untamed to shut it down. My feelings were hurt. I told her about the ring and my plans, and at a very high volume I should add. She countered with the obvious, that it was a stupid idea. She reminded me of the things that I had said to her in the past. We exchanged ugly names just before the ghetto exploded with the sounds of our rumble. Someone finally called the police.

I received sixteen stitches to my hand. I stopped the stab to my face with a punch. The knife ended up under a knuckle and broke that bone. I was not so innocent in the melee. I smashed everything that I could in her house and hit her as well, although not to kill. Neither one of us pressed charges.

My older brother Cenzo, a Police officer himself, picked me up at the hospital. The ride back to Staten Island was quiet until he said "There are real things worth fighting for out in this world Joie. I'm not going to tell you how to run your life, but never shed blood for something or someone that you don't love." I was overcome by a flood of emotion, not because of all that had happened, but because I realized that I had never truly fallen in love. I cried hard on Cenzo's shoulder, much to his discomfort.

The following summer, I signed up for anger management classes, in addition to physical therapy for my hand. All paid for by the ring I returned unscathed.

Mary called me almost a year later desperate to see me and for us to speak. I tried every which way to decline but I finally gave in when she offered to take the ferry to Staten Island to meet me, in the dead of winter. Nobody from outside of the island does that unless it is important. It had been almost a year since I left her at Jacobi Hospitals emergency room. Any thoughts of her after that were triggered by physical pain or headaches. I told her that I would meet her at her favourite pizza place on Seventh Avenue in the village instead.

I arrived early and sat at the table closest to the door. I was just watching the traffic and thinking that she had played me for a fool again, when she put her hand on my shoulder from behind. I stood up to face her, only to find a very swollen and pregnant woman standing in front of me. My shock showed and so she began to explain quickly. The Valentine's Day date that would end in the glorious end to us, not to mention my peace and tranquility, was with a man. It continued, clearly, and resulted in a pregnancy that he does not want to be a part of. None of that mattered to her, she went on to say, because she came to the conclusion that she was still in love with me. She dreamt of giving my little Corey a sibling. And she wanted us to be a family. My head was spinning. I could not believe her delusion and at the same time, her bullshit. My classes had done me well. I ordered her favourite pizza. She looked like a manatee swallowing it up. I asked her all of the pertinent questions like is every one healthy? Do you know the sex of the baby? How was she surviving?

She was living in an apartment in one of her Uncles homes, in Long Island, an apartment above his. The baby was a little girl. They were both healthy and she was due any day now. She was still awaiting approval for food stamps and welfare. We had a calm and mature discussion with even a few giggles. I left her smiling at the table while I went to an ATM machine and paid for our meal. When we walked outside, I hailed a cab and helped her in. I handed her two-hundred dollars and thanked her for thinking of me in her life plan. "I'm honoured." I said. "I wish you all of the best, but you and I should never have been." Her nose had widened so much from her pregnancy that her tears did not fall down her face. They just welled up above her nostrils.

A few weeks later Mary gave birth to Mariana, a beautiful and healthy baby girl. I was the only person to visit them in the hospital. I bought them some necessities and visited the baby often in the months to come. Mariana was enticing, but I realized I was doing them both an injustice by getting too close, so I slowly stopped my weekly trips there. As a result, Mary's phone calls became nasty and more like her former self. I counted to ten and put my training into play. The anger management classes paid off and my time with Mary became a valuable life lesson.

Divine intervention

11

The universe so powerful.

Two mortal beings. Magnetic pull.

Angels descend on silent wings.

Life transpires. Lovebirds sing.

I have chosen to spend a lot of time with family now. My little brothers have all grown up, while I wasn't watching, to become some of my best friends. Ironically, all of my experiences away from love, in search of love, had driven me back to love. The family kind.

We spent our summers surfing, laughing and creating havoc. My youngest brother Gianni had become an international model and star, at least in our eyes. He treated us to his fast and decadent lifestyle on occasion. "Beaches, babes and boats" was always his mantra. While I felt like a chaperone most of the time, I did enjoy the attention that being Gianni's sister now garnered. I brought him into my gay circles too. My little bro was funny and comfortable in his skin. The gay guys melted around him and my lesbian friends loved his crazy energy.

"I think I'm dyslexic." Gianni would tell me one glorious morning while packing the car for a day out on his boat. "Why do you think that? You would have been diagnosed by now. You're a college graduate. You have read and signed contracts for Pete's sake. How could you turn dyslexic?" I asked him. I laughed and we both stopped to think about his silly diagnosis. "Well, then I am having trouble with my eyes. I'm missing letters in words." "All right then I will drive." I replied with a wink. We both smiled and headed for the marina. He would schedule an appointment with an ophthalmologist for the following week. In the meantime, I had the pleasure of driving his bright yellow Seadoo Challenger all day.

Gianna complained about headaches and not seeing letters in print very often. I was sure that he just needed glasses and that he was fighting it.

His first doctors visit was inconclusive. "That just means I don't know, with a bow tie on." I would tell him. He had to stop driving now. Whatever was going on with him, it was progressing at a rapid rate. He was a beautiful mountain of a man with a vibrant personality to boot. It was hard to recognize that he was not feeling well. He would never let on. His three dimpled smile was a great camouflage.

The next diagnosis made sense to us. We actually celebrated the find. A doctor had concluded that his gargantuan neck muscles, and the weight exercises that he did to maintain it, was actually inhibiting flow to the brain. The pressure on nerves, major arteries, spinal fluid and just the base of the brain was causing the headaches and vision problems. He was prescribed both anti-inflammatory and anti-seizure medications. The gym and any exercise was a no, until he was back to normal. The subtle high and his compromised vision kept him home. Gianni lost the exuberance that he was well known for. We still laughed and joked incessantly when we were together but his time alone was now relegated to his computer.

It was the beginning of the internet era. AOL's *'You've got mail.'* was not yet annoying. New chat rooms, it seemed, were being created every day for every type of human being. It all served a purpose for Gianni. He was home bound waiting for the meds and rest to work. The headaches became unbearable and Mama started to seriously worry about him. I pushed Gianni to see a neurologist and to get several opinions.

I was just getting on a plane for a business trip when my baby brother called me. "Hey sis, how are you?" "I'm good." I replied "Just going to Miami overnight. What's going on?" "My doctor wants me to come in for the results of my tests." He had taken me up on my advice and had several very detailed appointments as a result. What we knew for sure was that the doctor who diagnosed the neck pressure was touted as a 'quack' by his peers. "That's great news. Call me when you know what the next steps are." I was excited about Gianni getting back to normal. He was twenty-six years old, stuck in his apartment and tied to his computer. "Well that's the thing." he went on to explain. "He wants me to bring a loved one with me. Can you come?" I knew in my heart that this was not good. The flight attendants were starting to ask everyone to turn off their cell phones and electronics in preparation for take off. "I'll be there bro. I'll be home tomorrow at five." I said. "I love you."

My work, the day, my trip home; it all dragged on like time, space and gravity was failing us on the planet. I addressed every morbid thought with a logical optimistic explanation. I am exceptionally good at this sort of life mathematics. The doctor could be asking for a loved one so that they could put this bullshit diagnosis and worry to bed, finally. Maybe Gianni was a head case and a hypochondriac. I was sure that the doctor wanted us to address the psychological reason he had manifested these headaches and vision issues. The time on his computer was further distorting his reality. We would have an honest discussion once I was back home and after this damn appointment. I had worked myself up for it all.

I noticed a slight twitch in his eye when I picked him up for the doctor's appointment. I didn't mention it because Gianni was ecstatic this morning. "I have met a great girl online Joie. And she is fucking drop dead gorgeous. We talked all night. Oh my God, I can't wait to meet her. Her name is Natalie. Isn't that a beautiful name? Are you listening to me?" These chat rooms had turned my brother into a chattering fool. "You don't meet someone online; you TALK to someone online." I corrected him. We were of a different generation. I loved and played in the physical world and he was becoming a virtual guy. It scared me. Not just for him, but for my son and the future of our species. "I feel like I met her." he said with a little boy voice. I would not argue with him on this trip to see the doctor. I was sure we would have a lot to discuss on our way back home. Like this chatting and his making himself sick.

Gianni put his arm around me as we left the doctors offices for the parking lot. He was smiling from ear to ear. It was a testament of his love that he was trying to cheer me up. I remained stoic only because I was rehearsing how to tell my Mama and the rest of the family this news.

My baby brother was finally and properly diagnosed with a brain tumor. The more serious news was that it was malignant and had metastasized, meaning that the cancer cells would make themselves at home throughout his body. The doctor was very logical. He proposed relief, quality of life and pain management before all else. They would schedule surgery to remove as much of the tumor in his head as possible, followed by radiation and chemo therapy to slow down the invasion. He still gave him six months to live. Did I mention he was only twenty-six years old? "I'm not scared." Gianni said, smiling brighter than anyone who had received such news should have. "I have my family. I have you Joie. And I have Natalie. I'm surrounded by love."

The family pulled together in one big positive push towards a miraculous outcome. Gianni had his surgery and while they removed most of it, they had to sever his optical nerve to do so. He was left blind but still smiling. His chat room relationships blossomed in that darkness. As much as it became crazier and crazier, who was I to take that joy away from him now. I moved in with Gianni to help him navigate this new life but he was truly brilliant at adaptation. I would come home to his recounting steps between furniture pieces and his stories of taking walks, where to, and exact step by step directions. He embraced this blind life wholeheartedly. I suppose he had no choice. 'The chemistry experiments' as he called him were horrible. The radiation caused severe bone pain and the headaches returned. The chemotherapy turned his stomach upside down. He could have lived with the nausea but it was the other end that made his life miserable. We spent hours in the bathroom together. If I wasn't rubbing away the pain of his constipation and gripe, I was cleaning up the mess of uncontrollable diarrhea, to his embarrassment. We would always laugh after the worst of it. "What kind of shit have you gotten me into." I said one night to make light of it all. He laid his head on my chest and stopped sniffling to laugh. "You know what is really horrible Joie?" "What, I said." automatically, but scared of his answer. "Your shit smells a hundred times worse when you're blind." "Try it. Next time you go. Close your eyes." Gianni fell asleep in my arms on the bathroom floor that evening and for many to come. He was right about the smell.

As the months passed and my brothers physical health deteriorated, so did his mental health, although unbeknownst to him. The darkness enveloped him and he found solace in it. His online relationship with Natalie flourished. They also spoke on the telephone often. Both professed their love in spite of never

ever sharing the same space or local air. Gianni refused to meet her. The agoraphobia was a by product of his blindness compounded by a side affect of his medications. He took forty-four pills per day at the height of his disease and that did not include the catheter in the middle of his chest, used for '*the chemistry experiment*'.

I took the time to get to know Natalie. I had to make sure she was real, an adult and not a lonely truck driver getting his rocks off at a stop down south in Alabama somewhere. She was indeed beautiful, both inside and out. She visited often, from the Toronto area, always so that we could devise a plan to surprise Gianni. She was in love with the man.

We were so comfortable with each other. If my miracle came to fruition, and Gianni survived this all, somehow, Natalie and I would be the best of friends and sisters in law. She was funny, caring, smart, unpretentious, gentle and hot! How could the universe give him all of this to look forward to and yet take away his vision to see it, as well as his longevity to live it? I would ask myself that question often. What was the master plan?

"It's already written." Gianni opined while we smoked some of his medical marijuana together, while laying on the floor side by side. "Expand on that." I laughed. "Well, older sibling." Giggle "We are beings of the story. Already written and archived in the universal library of all beings. You may think that you're rewriting the story, changing a sentence or path, here and there. But even that has been written." "Fascinating novel." I said. "The protagonist is falsely empowered." We laughed so hard. We tried to have these conversations with British accents. "They don't work with Spanish accents." He would say. I had some of the best conversations and times of my life with this man, my beautiful baby brother.

We were all happy beyond words when Sloan Kettering called. Gianni had a donor match for a complete bone marrow transplant. We packed him up quickly and sent him there by ambulance. He had called Natalie and bridged me on. I think we all cried happy tears.

The treatment would require that he be given uber dosages of both chemotherapy and radiation before introducing the new bone marrow that would take hold and heal him. I wanted more time with him. The sixth month mark was upon us and he was at his worst, although still so jovial and committed to his recovery. He called me often from SK. He was quarantined and I guess felt alone without me there. Natalie was also not at his fingertips on the computer. Gianni was scared and lonely although he never really complained. He would just call to speak to me about the oddest of things. "Did you know that human toes will fuse one day because we don't use them? We will have one big toe! I don't think open toe heels will be sexy anymore, when that happens Joie." was one of his many calls.

He wasn't feeling well he had told me on one of the twenty calls I received on that last day of November. They had connected him to a new drip. Antibiotics. So his transplant would be delayed at least ten days. He was anxious and I asked him to relax. "Call Natalie." I said. She had a way of calming him down. I was slightly annoyed when he called me back less than an hour later. I was on the other line with work and had already spoken to him so many times. "Gianni please call Natalie. I'm on the other line with a problem at work." I could hear him breathing. "All right." He said sadly. "Are you okay?" I would manage to ask quickly. "Yes. Just wanted to ask you a question but it can wait." We both said I love you and I resigned to call him later or tomorrow morning.

The phone rang at two in the morning on December 1st. It was his doctor at the hospital telling me that my baby brother had passed away. I couldn't breathe, I could not speak. I heard myself replying in a hum while holding back the scream. I had made my way downstairs to the kitchen table, while she spoke, and I proceeded to flip it over, in a rage, as soon as I hung up the telephone. I didn't call him back dammit! "WHY?" I screamed out loud, looking up at my ceiling. My tears nearly drowned me twice before I could compose myself to call Mama and everyone else. By five in the morning I had only one last call to make and I really thought I could do so without crying again. I called Natalie. She was calming for me to hear. We both cried a bit but something happened on that call. It did not feel like an ending as much as it did a beginning. I would not recognize that little nuance until many years later. I ended the call promising to give her details of the funeral and for us to have our own celebration of his life. He would leave this dimension without ever meeting Natalie face to face, but still so full of love for her.

Gianni was big on celebrating birthdays. He always made a big deal out of them. We carefully planned our gifts to each other as part of a theme. His twenty seventh physical year on earth would have been on the day after Christmas. It was a difficult day for me but Natalie and I consoled each other through it. She had our sense of humour. She made me laugh like he did and I made her laugh like he did. We would comfort each other through the holidays altogether but it was my fortieth birthday on January eighth that was going to be the most difficult without him.

We met in Miami to not only celebrate my birthday but to also toast my mountain man baby brother. The hotel room that we shared on Ocean Drive was sexy. Although this appeared to be the perfect weekend date, I was very cognizant of her being my sister in law and my brothers recent passing. Thoughts of her, in typical Joie fashion, made me feel icky and worse, disloyal to my brother.

The party was hearty without a doubt. Natalie and I turned Miami upside down. We drank excessively and laughed constantly. She was a great girl. I kept saying that to myself in my head. And she was beautiful.

She is of South Asian decent, an island near India. Her skin is the colour of cinnamon, which just happens to be the biggest product and industry from that island, known as Sri Lanka. Jet black long hair, dark eyes, long eyelashes, perfectly heart shaped lips and a smile that will warm you. Gianni only saw her in pictures. He would have melted to hear her laugh in person. It is a classy and sexy laugh that you can feel, and not just hear. Tall and thick, beyond all of that, she truly is an exotic beauty.

I tried to get her interested in some of the men while we were out. None blew her hair back, but it was still early, only a month after his death. I tried to make the constant incoming thoughts of her go away as well. It was all very proper that weekend in January but Gianni was reaching out to us from another dimension.

Natalie started to receive messages from beyond that without question were from Gianni. Whether through friends or mediums, she knew that no one would know the content of their intimate conversations, not even me. She also didn't feel completely comfortable in sharing any of this with me. Meanwhile, I was having dreams of her, and of my brother speaking to me. He kept urging me to look past his relationship and love for her. He was insistent that we get together. The one speed bump that he did not account for in his ghost thin plan was that Natalie was a straight woman, and well, that I was not.

I decided to disperse of the crazy thoughts by speaking about them out loud, like therapy. I called Natalie to share what was happening to me. It was also part warning, to stay away from me, but the conversation did not go as planned. Once again, we found compatibility in our conversation. We were both going through the same exact thing but in different ways. Could we both be crazy? If so, something was still pulling us together. I believed in much of what she told me. After all, I grew up the grandchild of a Santeria high priestess. It was my loyalty to my brother that made it wrong, but I was weakening with every one of our conversations. There was definitely a power bringing us together.

By the time I told her of my business trip in Toronto, on February fifth, we were craving to touch each other. Our talks had definitely changed. I no longer saw her as a sister in law but as someone who was meant for me to pursue. I remembered Gianni's thoughts about *'the book being written.'* It all came to make sense when I started to accept it logically.

She had left me a very cheeky voice mail message while I was at work, just before that trip. It said "Joie, I give you my cunt scent to do anything you want to do to me while you're here in Toronto." It wasn't what she said, so much, as how she said it; in a voice that made every hair on your body stand at attention. I packed my bags for a business trip that would change my life forever, and in another country.

I tested her allegiance to her heterosexuality by asking her to kiss me at the airport. She did not hesitate. Natalie and I kissed for the very first time on February 5th, 2000. It was perfect and somewhat confusing to me. I had never experienced feeling a kiss above the waist. I had spent a lifetime being a groin kisser, much to my emotional disappointment. She won't know this until she reads this passage, but I almost cried that day. That first kiss made my heart skip a beat. It is not a sentimental Hallmark card creation. I am here to tell you that it is quite real and worth the wait.

I am not a musician but kissing has a marked time much like I think can be measured by a metronome. There is a natural rate that we each have and when it compliments, we make music together. You cannot force it, or correct it, it just occurs.

Such was the music and love that Natalie and I made on that first date. I won't write about orgasms, positions, how hard or how gently we went at it. That would detract from how extraordinary it was to be in a woman's arms, devouring her body, and to finally feel something emotionally.

That this was truly heaven sent, if we all believe what transpired to bring her and I together, only made it all feel even more miraculous.

We left the hotel room once to have an official date dinner. It was flawless if you disregard my clumsiness and that I spilled my drink. She never flinched and just smiled at me lovingly.

I did come to Toronto for business so it made sense that we would part on Sunday and be responsible grown ups on Monday morning. I invited her back for lunch on Monday afternoon. It was hard to let her go.

The pizza and drinks were delivered to my room as planned. Natalie arrived looking absolutely gorgeous in her professional attire. We enjoyed our meal and succumbed to the sexual tension, that inexplicable magnetism between us. Her kisses were the perfect combination of tender and dirty.

I think she picked up on my sadness as we dressed to return to our work. I fully assessed the magnitude of what we had opened ourselves up to. We were from two different countries, two different cultures and most glaring, from two different sexualities. If you factored in that we were brought together by the spirit of my dead brother, it seemed totally crazy to continue. Something so perfect marred by such daunting details.

"Can I be your secret lover?" she asked, cutting the silence and sadness between us. "Sure." I answered that not knowing what would be our future, covert or otherwise. That afternoon before she left me with another delicious kiss, I gave Natalie a simply made Inuit ring that I had purchased at the hotel gift shop. While it was for her to wear, it would really turn out to be my affirmation. *I'll be back to see you. To fall more deeply and madly in love with you.* These words were not uttered but the ring was my unspoken promise.

You sang to me

12

The sweetest of all sounds is the voice of someone you love.

I think back to all of the Jacque Cousteau shows that I watched as a child, even my Saturday morning Mutual of Omaha episodes, and never did I envision my traveling to Canada. No Latina in her right mind would head farther North.

I returned to Toronto in March, exactly a month later, and every month after that. Sometimes, I made the trip twice a month. I was now traveling from Florida or various beautiful Caribbean islands, from wherever my work would take me. Natalie and I were falling deeply in lust and madly in love.

Long distance relationships are not for the weak or insecure. At any given time even the most confident human being will experience random bouts of both. I had great moments of exhaustion and she questioned it all, including her new sexuality, often.

I have been told that in times of stress we revert to habit. Natalie's habit was the chat rooms. She had also found comfort in them over the years. Ours was a stressful relationship for her, back then. I know that now but early in our love, I didn't understand. We were inseparable and perfectly happy when we were physically together but she was online when we were apart. She hated being alone while I was traveling the world. And she was still addressing her sexuality.

Every year, several times a year, I would whisk her away to some beautiful part of the world, renew our excitement in each other and bring her back home to Canada. Then I would return to the monthly visits. At all times we had incredible sex for days on end and satisfied every 'relationship healthy' fantasy that either of us have craved. Insert note here: avocado can cause extreme itching. The va-jay-jay is not a place for guacamole, but I digress once again.

To write, in depth, of our difficulties at that time would only serve to emphasize that which we worked hard to overcome. There will be no juicy tidbits of our relationship released herein, unless I think they can help someone else. I will only say that the most perfect adventures come with skinned knees and bloody lips.

We were nine years into to this long distance love fest and struggle to be together combo when Natalie awoke having had enough. She gave me an ultimatum in 2009 to conclude my business in the United States, pack my shit, and finally live with her full time in Canada. I knew she was serious. For the record, this was not a booty call for me. I was seriously and fully committed to our relationship. I don't know if I could have gone on forever like this but I had certainly resigned to it being my life. I had until the end of the year, almost twelve months, to make it happen or lose her forever. I set on the path to that goal without question. Now here is the lesson, my lesson to be exact. I did not inform her of what I was doing to that end or along the way. Life went on for us without her hearing of my plans.

The truth is that I was selling my business and preparing my family for my move. Corey was now married and I had Grandchildren. It was not difficult but still a process. A process that Natalie should have been privy to, but that I wanted to somehow surprise her with.

My world was dramatically changed in the summer of 2009 when Natalie broke up with me. We had had arguments throughout the nine years, of course, and half ass parted ways. There were a few weekend break ups that I can remember. I had given my *'I'm done'* speech more times than I cared to remember too, but we never stopped communicating. This time she was different. The correct word would be adamant. "I can't be with you anymore Joie." She told me on the telephone. "Please respect my wishes. Do not call me or contact me in any way. Don't make this harder on me. I need to find myself and I am through with us." It came suddenly and with every sentence I could hear the same drum that was played in *'The Ten Commandments'* when Moses is banned from Egypt and his name is stricken from every pillar. I was scheduled to fly out to Singapore in two days. I was sure this break-up, out of nowhere, was hormonal. As far as I was concerned, we had plans to live together and I was working towards that, but I didn't say so. Even when she banned me from Egypt like Moses, I choked!

I was heartbroken but confident that all would pass. The trip to Singapore was important. I would email her or call her from the other side of the world. Better yet, I was sure she would miss me.

I called and emailed Natalie many times, while traveling, but she ignored me. The easiest way for me to survive this was to stay busy. I ran myself ragged so that sleep would come quickly. I stayed in the area; Malaysia, Asia, and Indonesia. I wanted to respect her wishes with the hope that she would miss me. I did send her pictures via email like *'Where in the world is Carmen San Diego.'*. Joie in Mumbai, Joie in Hong Kong, Joie in Singapore, Joie in Jakarta, Joie in Tokyo. When she finally replied she broke my heart in two. After nine years together, surfing some big waves, but staying on our board together, Natalie was dating someone else. Correction, several others. She had never truly dated she told me. She went from a sad marriage, to talking to Gianni, to divorce and on to me. Once again, she needed to find herself. All of it would have been easy to understand had I been reading a book, but it was devastating to my life.

Not only was everything I owned or did involved in my process to relocate, but I was thousands of miles away from anyone that could hug me through this.

It only took a couple of nights of excessive drinking in some sleazy Malaysian clubs, getting lap danced by a Philippine trans women, to help me think straight.

I would fly back to New York to find comfort in my friends and family. I would still move forward with the relocation in hopes of winning her back. New York to Toronto is a puddle jumping flight. It would not be a culture shock, I thought.

I did go on some dates of my own when I returned to the states. All were disappointing. I realized I was tired of dating. The act of being on and charming for someone who could be shady, stopped being fun when I was no longer shady myself. I had always prided myself on being honest but if I am to be so with myself, I was poontang driven. Yes, there is another ugly word for the glorious hoo-ha derived from the Latin word for stinking.

It was after a stinking date in New York that I sent Natalie an email and a song clip, 'On the Ocean' by K'Jon. The lyrics were about our ship coming in and how I had to be strong. I really thought that she would ignore it too but she finally called me, almost six weeks after our break-up.

"I love the song." Her voice melted me. I was so afraid of saying the wrong thing. If nothing else, I would work hard to maintain our friendship. She had been my best friend for nine years. It was on that call that I realized this. We poured our hearts out. There was nothing to lose at this point. I had not spoken to her for six weeks after nine years of doing so every day, sometimes several times a day, not including our time together.

She told me about her dates, all men. Natalie had not embraced her lesbianism back then. Dating men was all she knew and she had not dated many. I listened to my friend without judging or jealousy. I was genuinely proud of her courage. When we finished telling each other all that we had missed for those six weeks I said "Why am I not part of your dating pool? I understand you're trying to find yourself. Why does that not include me? Please let me take you out. No relationship stress. Just a date with Joie." She said yes.

I hung up the telephone and jumped up to fist pump the air in every direction. The one thing that I had mastered over the many years of my life was dating. We made plans for me to come up to Toronto in September. I would stay at a hotel nearby. No pressure on either of us. I longed to see my friend. The lover part would either happen or not.

I failed to mention that in the middle of all of this traveling and the break up, I was training for a duathlon. I was in the best shape of my life. She had not seen for six weeks of my most intense training minus the couple of days drinking at the strip club. At this point in my life I was swimming forty-four laps in an Olympic size pool and riding 15.3 miles on a bike, each on alternating days. I felt buff and was solid. I would flaunt it a little on our first date in a long time.

I was scheduled to meet Natalie for tea and coffee upon my arrival and before going to my hotel but my flight was delayed going up. By the time I landed, picked up my rental car and drove to her house it was after midnight. She asked me to pick her up for a quick hello anyway, before checking in to the Hilton nearby. She was more beautiful than ever when she came out although limping. She had injured herself playing volleyball. We parked in a nearby lot to giggle and say hello but it wasn't long before we were making out in my car. Still, we kept it simple and I took her back home after that nice surprise.

The next day I picked her up in the afternoon after my swimming exercise at the hotel. I was still in training. It was an exceptionally warm early September in Toronto and I wore shorts and a moderately tight t shirt. She noticed right away. Although we tried to pace ourselves, Natalie and I ended up in bed together that entire weekend except for the part where I took her out to dinner.

Our dinner date was magical. We talked so much and laughed so hard. We held hands, may be even kissed. My point is that it was perfect for both of us. One of the things we discussed was the ultimatum and what I had been doing to meet her love demands. "Why didn't you tell me?" she asked. "I wanted to get it done and surprise you." We still talk about the stupidity of the that silent & strong move.

I was supposed to leave on Tuesday but I accompanied her to the doctor for her injury only to find out that she had broken her ankle. I stayed to take care of her and have been here ever since. I did go to the states to pick up my things and put some minor things in order.

We were legally married on February 5th, 2010, exactly 10 years after that first kiss and more at the airport in Toronto. We had a big bash and celebration later that year in August. Natalie walked down the aisle to 'On the Ocean' by K'Jon at that ceremony. Fifty-five of our closest friends and family attended. I don't know that they are all aware of our journey to that day. They certainly don't know my adventures, until this book.

I used to think that life had not been kind to me. Today I know it to be quite the opposite. I have had exactly the right amount of turmoil, loss, pain and hard knocks that made me the person that Natalie fell in love with. More to that point, it is because of all of that drama and trauma, that I now know that love is actually the Holy Grail. We take great pride and make a huge effort to treat each other well and with kindness. We are blessed by the many angels that brought us together. More than I have mentioned in this book. I intend to marry her over and over again if she agrees.

Salsa dancing is the vertical representation of a horizontal desire, much like a relationship is a combined representation of love and understanding. There is a correlation. Stick with me please.

In both dancing and love:

Don't turn her too much.
If she loses step, you catch up.
Don't lose hold.
And lastly, put both you heart and your hips into it.

Redamancy

(n.) the act of loving the one who loves you; a love returned in full.

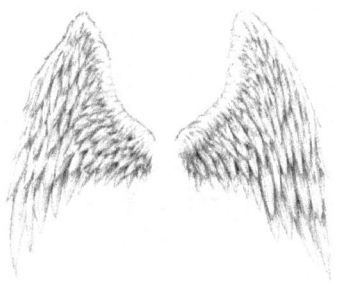

The book was written, as an angel once told me, long before my birth. Who we will be, over several lifetimes, has already been defined. We cannot rewrite nor erase any chapters in our life, no matter how painful or confusing. They are lessons. The stars will always light the way for us to find our person. The universe thrives on creating love that lasts forever.

The End.

About the Author

Joie Lamar made her way to Canada 22 years ago, from the United States, when she met the love of her life. They were married in Ontario, Canada in 2010. She is most passionate about equal rights for all human beings, celebrating the many heroes and she-roes of the LGBTQ community and loving our animal friends.

Salsa Hips is volume 2 of her Lips & Hips memoir series. Mambo Lips ©, volume 1, was released in March, 2015 and is currently a best seller being considered for film.

"My head is full of poetry and writing ideas. I don't write because I want to, I write because I have to." "This is my happily ever after part of life."

See Whores

By Joie Lamar
February 2022

See Whores is a compulsively readable psychological thriller, and volume 2 of a 3 part crime series, written by Joie Lamar. It is almost impossible to put down, and begins with a warning that is most apropos for a well written story with many depictions of abuse and graphic violence. That said, it is one of See Whores fascinating characters, Isabel, that keeps readers intrigued. She is brilliant, beautiful, and has survived a tortured past. How can her many dark truths help Detective Dan Cordova stop a vicious serial killer from murdering street workers in the city that never sleeps? As Ms. Lamar describes this novel "Expect a mindfuck!"

www.ingramcontent.com/pod-product-compliance
Lightning Source LLC
Chambersburg PA
CBHW070914080526
44589CB00013B/1284